PROCESS THIS

PROCESS THIS

*Undergraduate Writing
in Composition Studies*

NANCY C. DEJOY

UTAH STATE UNIVERSITY PRESS
Logan, Utah

Utah State University Press
Logan, Utah 84322–7800

Manufactured in the United States of America
Cover design by Barbara Yale-Read

Library of Congress Cataloging-in-Publication Data

DeJoy, Nancy C., 1958–
  Process this : undergraduate writing in composition studies / Nancy DeJoy.
    p. cm.
  Includes bibliographical references and index.
  ISBN 0–87421–595–1 (alk. paper)
  1. English language–Rhetoric–Study and teaching. 2. Report writing–Study and teaching
(Higher) I. Title.
  PE1404.D388 2004
  808'.042'0711—dc22
                                2004015505

CONTENTS

This book is dedicated in loving memory to
JAMES A. BERLIN
and
ROBERT W. DEJOY SR.
who helped me learn the value of a life of meaningful work.

ACKNOWLEDGMENTS

Many people have been supportive of the work that appears in these pages. The faculty of my undergraduate program at Nazareth College encouraged me early on to challenge accepted theories and practices during my introduction to the field of rhetoric and composition. I especially thank Dr. Deborah Dooley, Dr. Monica Weis, and Dr. Alex Sutherland for their support at that time in my life. I also thank Krista Ratcliffe and Janice Lauer for writing letters of recommendation for my sabbatical, and Millikin University for granting me the sabbatical that gave me time to write this book. Janice also read an early version of chapter one; her comments were much appreciated. The support of Millikin's Nyberg Grants for faculty development and scholarship related to teaching also contributed to this work by supplying time and resources for me to work with other faculty in the first-year writing program to create collaborative approaches to curriculum building. Randy Brooks, the chair of the English Department at Millikin, has celebrated every stage of the process as I waited for final approval of this project; for that I thank him. Irwin "Bud" Weiser read versions of early chapters and was encouraging at every step; his support is at the heart of my ability to believe in this project at the earliest stages and most difficult times. The reviewers of this manuscript were generous and encouraging in their responses. I thank them for their time and for listening so carefully to this text.

Nancy Bragg introduced me to service learning in ways that fostered integrated approaches to teaching, service, research, and scholarship. In doing so, she changed the course of my thinking about the teaching of first-year writing and helped me to create stronger connections between that work and my community literacy work. For this she has my deepest gratitude. Nancy also introduced me to my community partners at Project READ in Decatur. Vicki Harbeck and Dianne DeVore were so welcoming and so willing to work together toward shared goals for all of our students that much of the success of my work in this area is owed to them.

Many students, colleagues, and friends contributed to this book. Nicole Cassidy, Jennifer Eason, Kathy Klemesrud, Travis Meisenheimer, Linda Osborne, Carrie Owens, and Meg Schleppenbach added much to an analysis of the empirical data that appears in chapter one. Linda and Nicole also spent time doing a final reading of the book; their comments have made the work clearer. Bonnie Gunzenhauser and Rosemarie King generously agreed to teach the curriculum discussed in chapter three and did much to enhance that curriculum as we worked together to integrate reading into the first-semester courses in new ways. Bonnie also read numerous versions of this manuscript; her comments and her belief in this project sustained me throughout the process. Her friendship over the past five years has reintroduced me to the joys of teaching, travel, and research and has given me renewed self-confidence. Ed and Mary Yonan also read chapters as they were written; their insightful and intelligent responses inspired me to remember the larger educational context for my work. Beth Hoger sent letters of support and sabbatical treats that greatly enriched my research and writing time. Denise Myers made time to listen as I worked through difficult points. Linda Osborne and Cindy Giesing instituted "Nancy Night" during my sabbatical. Every Thursday they would cook a great meal with food that was beyond my sabbatical budget, open a bottle of wine, and listen to what I had written that week. Their commitment to this project, and to the ideas of participation and contribution that form its core, created a home for my work. Erica Frisicaro, Katie Malcolm, and Karl Stolley, previous undergraduate students who are now in the field, have given me concrete ways to understand the importance of my work in their lives and in the field. All of these students, colleagues, and friends spent hours listening and responding to my ideas. In fact, all of the undergraduate students I have shared classrooms with over the past eight years have supported this work in one way or another, often generously agreeing to try new things and to take risks with their own ideas and assignments. Although they are too numerous to name, I thank each of them here, especially Christopher Bronke, Elizabeth Ledman, Susan Barco, Mary Ellen Paley, and Jenny Medden Giesler.

I also thank my mother, Cecilia DeJoy, for all of her interest in this project. Even though she has been busy pursuing her own undergraduate education, she has maintained a serious interest in my progress and has made space for my work in her home during my visits. All of my brothers and sisters, Susan, Sheryl, Bob, Pat, Dave, Dan, and Brian also made room in their lives to discuss my work and its progress.

Finally, I would like to thank Michael Spooner for all of his direction and support throughout the submission, revision, and publication process. His directness, enthusiasm, and attention were more thoughtful and encouraging than this first-time book author could have ever hoped for.

Experience is not practice.
JULIA KRISTEVA

Activity is not practice.
MICHEL PECHEUX

INTRODUCTION

Discussions about the place and function of student writing have informed composition studies since the rise of the process movement in American higher education. As Sondra Perl notes in her introduction to *Landmark Essays on Writing Process*, this discussion was informed early on by empirical approaches that centered student writing processes as objects of inquiry. These studies often identified conflicts between and among the accounts of writing processes narrated by professional writers, those put forth in textbooks, and those observed in student writers (xii-xiii). What happened to the texts produced by the students in these scenarios is unclear. This lack of clarity about the relationship between the products of student writing and the field still pervades too much of our work. The resulting silences position students of our writing classes—especially our first-year writing classes—too strongly as consumers, too clearly as adapting to, rather than participating in and contributing to, composition studies. I begin here from a moment in time (the 1990s) when many compositionists were beginning to struggle toward redefinitions of student writer subjectivity that challenged this unequal positioning of members of the writing classes in relation to the field and its practices. I look at and move forward from that point in time as a person who saw the practice of teaching undergraduate students as a serious part of participating in and contributing to that struggle.

As Stephen Parks explains in *Class Politics: The Movement for Students' Right to Their Own Language*, the configuration of composition studies that centered process while marginalizing the products of student writing became institutionalized, in large part, in the 1970s and 1980s through our professional organizations. Parks illustrates the ways that the version of students' right to their own language (SRTOL), favored by the Modern Language Association (MLA), National Council of Teachers of English (NCTE) and the Conference on College Composition and Communication

(CCCC), assumed individualistic notions of rights and language over more community-based and activist approaches to writing pedagogies and classroom practices (249–50). *Class Politics* is smart work in many ways, especially because it exposes that the process movement began a trajectory that led us to center internal conflicts as the business of composition studies. Read in this way, the history of composition studies emerges as an imperative within which professional discourses and the texts created by students can be kept apart from one another in significant ways. At the heart of the matter for Parks is the fact that the profession chose this path over the New University Conference (NUC) resolution that would have centered more political and social versions of the SRTOL movement, versions that would have challenged conceptions of composition studies as separate from progressive organizations and movements outside of the traditional structures of academia. Such a focus would have been based on

> a professional perspective that understands the writing classroom as one point within a larger system of social and class oppression. Without a [professional] organization which creates connections between such scholars and political organizations, however, the critical mass needed to affect such possibilities in the definition of the writing teacher could not occur.[1] (209)

But this moment also marks a serious and defining set of decisions about the place and functions of undergraduate student discourses in the profession. For as Parks notes, SRTOL was part of a larger activist movement "that would focus on the student as a participant within the discipline of English" and, in the end, this was the "contentious question" that MLA, NCTE, and CCCC managed to write out of their SRTOL statements (71). In other words, the major professional organizations of the discipline set aside the issues of student agency and subjectivity as constructive in and of English studies, replacing them with arguments about the values of standard English given "the way things are." Ultimately, the repression of student agency in the struggles that led to the formalized SRTOL statement failed to position anything other than middle-class white English as constituting the history of English in America. Parks states:

That is, in a resolution and a document clearly initiated by NUC activists to speak on behalf of African American and working-class students, it would appear that there is little demonstration of what their culture, language, or history represents about the historical development of English in the United States (186)

in the SRTOL statement. Within this frame, "the SRTOL language statement creates an image of dialects as a cultural problem which can be solved by the raised consciousness of its citizens" and "economic concerns are cast primarily in light of how to expand acceptable dialects within corporate capitalism, not how to use dialects to question it" as was the original intent of the NUC's resolution (184). Using Black English as his case study, Parks shows how the rewritten SRTOL document "does not offer positive models of Black English's impact on standard American English," thereby constituting the dialects of Black English, and "non-standard" forms of the language more generally, as the "other" of English studies (186). From this point of view, inclusion of the "other" in "the way things are" takes the place of critiquing and revising the structures of discrimination that allow a false story of the history of English in America to stand as truth in order to construct a notion of a "standard" that rests upon the exclusion of the ways the "other" has, in fact, participated in and contributed to the construction of American English. One can then argue that standardization is necessary to inclusion, even as one argues that the acceptance of "other" dialects is, in and of itself, an important and noble cause.

It is not surprising that letting students tell their own stories in their own voices becomes a valued pedagogy at this stage in our history. But as Parks illustrates, this value is, sometimes overtly and sometimes through implication, a reaction against more radical views of the profession and of language, views that would 1) revise the false assumptions about who participated in and contributed to the history of English in America, and 2) define the writing classroom as a place where the inequities resulting from these false assumptions are addressed and challenged. This is why SRTOL had to work toward a position that defined language, and particularly standard English, as the source of access to resources and power, claiming that anyone who used that form of English—regardless of race, class, gender, or ethnicity could become "equal" in American democracy.[2] That is, students' and many teachers' roles in the writing classroom and in society more generally were restricted in particular ways, ways that favored adaptation to and consumption of standards and process "models" that favored those standards.

Within this frame, the distinction between process and product takes on particular forms. The process, no matter what it manifests is, in and of itself, somehow liberatory. The product, especially its place and function in the discursive field from which it emerges, is irrelevant. But this can only happen because that field itself, composition studies, and its concerns do not emerge as the content of the course. Process itself becomes course content. In "Paralogic Hermeneutic Theories, Power, and the Possibility for Liberating Pedagogies," Sidney Dobrin explains the problem this way: "Even in the most politically savvy classrooms, process is generally taught by simply reinscribing knowledge, by perpetuating process thinking, by perpetuating inscribed methods of inquiry. . . . Students learn to repeat strategies (138–39). Dobrin later clarifies the consequences of centering process in the writing classroom in this way. "This activity means only learning the processes of a particular dominant discourse and simply reinscribing sets of processes. In many ways, this activity is exactly the sort of oppressive education against which liberatory pedagogies work" (139–40). Student writers and their texts cannot concern themselves with the assumptions, false or otherwise, about the discipline because other matters define the content of the products that emerge from student writing. It is not merely the language of process and or English that is standardized here, but a concept of student subjectivity that maintains students' positions as consumers of the field.

The tensions created by centering students' discourses in the classroom but disenfranchising those discourses in the discipline itself emerge as a defining feature of what I will refer to throughout this book as first-phase process model movements. While I will discuss these tensions at length in chapter one, it is important to remember that I am not using the term "first-phase" to designate a time period or a logical sequence. To treat the history or future of composition studies as a linear progression from one stage to another with definitive breaks between and among those stages would be a mistake. Instead, I use the term "first-phase" in a way similar to that used by Elaine Showalter when she explains the stages of feminist literary criticism in her introduction to *The New Feminist Criticism: Essays on Women, Literature, and Theory.* Showalter outlines three stages of feminist criticism. The first stage "concentrated on exposing the misogyny of literary practices, the literary abuse or textual harassment of women in classic and popular literature, and the exclusion of women from literary history" (5). The second stage "was the discovery that women writers had a literature of their own, whose historical and thematic coherence, as well as artistic importance, had been obscured by the patriarchal values that dominated our culture" (6). This stage led to "a massive recovery and rereading of literature by women of all nations and historical periods" (6). In its third stage, feminist criticism "demanded not just the recognition of women's writing but a radical rethinking of the conceptual grounds of literary study, a revision of the accepted theoretical assumptions about reading and writing" (8). Showalter is clear that these stages occur simultaneously, sometimes in integrated ways and other times as separate endeavors, and the essays in the collection exemplify each type and invite readers to conceptualize the relationships between and among them. This is not a matter of leaving things behind, but of moving between and among available methodologies with a purpose. First-phase does not refer to a historical time period, or to a single approach as we are used to distinguishing between and among those approaches (e.g., expressivist, cognitivist, etc.). Instead, first-phase writing process models as I define them here are those that bracket student subjectivity in ways that make it difficult for students and their discourses to become active agents in the field.

The fact is that there are components of those models that we cannot identify with as we attempt to revise a historical trajectory that brackets student subjectivity in this way. The ways that those models challenge the over-valorization of explication, the ways that they improve the status of student discourses in the classroom and in the work of professionals in the field, the ways that they value student voices are not merely precursors to some "new" model. Rather, they are both analytic concepts that expose ideologies about writers and writing and generative ideas around which the field creates practices. The tendency to use different heuristics for the analytic and generative work of the field than those we hold out as appropriate for use by students becomes a serious issue if we wish to create more inclusive concepts of writing and of student writers within a process frame.

Throughout the course of this project, I have become increasingly convinced that while reading the process movement in this different way does not fit into the categories we usually use to tell that story, it is, nonetheless, vital to understanding the potential for more inclusive disciplinary practices that emerge in contemporary revisions to process theories, pedagogies, and practices. I engage in a critical relationship with current revisions to those models for the purpose of re-imagining the ways that we position student writers and student texts in relation to composition studies. This work, then, is an attempt to open spaces in which participation and contribution—rather than adaptation and consumption—can become defining features of the relationships between and among members of the writing classes who constitute composition studies.

The need for rethinking the field in light of this hope and purpose is most clearly outlined by Susan Miller in her 1991 book, *Textual Carnivals: The Politics of Composition.* Miller is particularly relevant here because she acknowledges the importance of remembering that

> the prominent work of Mina Shaughnessey and of various process theorists like Linda Flower and Bartholomae has demonstrated [that] the prospect of theorizing composition instruction in terms of student learning and actual student writing has persistently captured the imagination and respect of many who otherwise doubt the "intellectual content" of the field [including many who teach in the field]. Consequently, the identity of the student in teaching, research, and administrative practices offers a key to the politics of composition in every issue considered here. (195)

Toward the end of *Textual Carnivals*, Miller outlines the two main ways that compositionists have projected their "posture toward their others" (181) since the more conservative versions of students' language won out in the struggles Parks outlines as defining the professionalization of the teaching of writing in the 1960s and 70s. The first "posture" is to correct "how composition is ignored, trivialized, unequal and otherwise marginalized in comparison to more privileged departmental, collegiate, institutional, and social surroundings." The goal here is to make composition "equal to its sister studies . . . [by] explaining unrecognized intellectual (if not ideological) connections between composition and literature, which could become two parallel strains in one disciplinary home . . ." (181). The second "posture", which "the 'process paradigm' and empirical methods have highlighted is fundamentally separatist" (182). This posture aligns composition studies with "established social scientific research methods in cognitive psychology and ethnography and stresses links to research in established humanistic fields such as historical rhetoric and linguistics" (182). Miller criticizes "both the integrationist and the separatist moves because neither has worked on the fundamental structure that necessitates them" (183). She concludes that

> both separatists and integrationists inadvertently reinforce their alienation by defending and maintaining the 'studentness' of a particular kind of writing, precisely *as* the student's right. Keeping student writing in its place keeps composition studies in its place stably inside its regulated frameworks of inconsequentiality. (183–184)

That is, the internal fight suppresses and is restricted by the absence of considerations about the place of student discourse in the profession. To overcome this double bind, Miller proposes that we need "a genuine alternative that would further require questions and answers about human results for both students and composition professionals in their divisions, definitions, and new intellectual movements" (186). She concludes that "powerful attitudes toward student writers and unprivileged writing inevitably control the status of composition studies, its relations to those outside it, and its self-image and ways of working out its new professionalization" (195). In 2000, Stephen North illustrated the ways that Miller's insights apply to graduate studies in English, concluding in *Refiguring the Ph. D. in English Studies* that

> all sorts of commentators, graduate faculty in particular, will propose changes in just about everything else—different readings, different graduate classroom practices, different teacher-training programs, shorter time to degree, and so on: anything, anything, anything other than giving doctoral students greater license in terms of what they might write. (260)

Like others in the field who are struggling toward opening spaces for contribution and participation to all members of the writing classes, North notes that the role of student writing is a key factor in such struggles. North is willing to be fairly aggressive about how to change the status of student discourses, but even the pedagogical approach he outlines as part of that struggle can fail to reposition student writing as vital to the profession if it fails to see students' and teachers' initial attempts as anything other than a starting place—a transition toward more inclusive practices (166).[3]

As I will illustrate in the early chapters of this book, recent responses to the devalued position of undergraduate student writers and student writing have tended to leap over the relationship between these issues and the field itself in their attempts to revise composition studies. Three major revisionary trends in first-year writing illustrate this point: the turn toward cultural criticism, the turn toward community-based literacy activities, and the turn toward audiences outside of the field. Despite their tendency to bracket the profession as a forum for undergraduate student writing, however, some of these revisions to process-based approaches to first-year writing do value participation and contribution outside of the field as appropriate goals of pedagogy and appropriate purposes for student writing. In cultural studies approaches, critique drives the move away from consumption. In service learning approaches, community-based literacy work drives the move away from consumption. In social process approaches, the move toward student discourses that take relevant readers outside of the classroom as an audience drives the move away from consumption. Ultimately, I argue, these revisions have excluded students from participating in the field of composition studies itself, thereby making it difficult for writing teachers and students to move away from models of consumption and adaptation.

Examining and understanding the contradictions between theory and practice that create, and are created by, these unequal notions of writing subjectivity is critical to redefining undergraduate student writers and their texts as part of our field, as subjects rather than as objects. It would be impossible to change the field in any significant way without acknowledging and working to revise the unequal relationships that drive a situation in which literacy is, by definition, primarily an act of consumption and adaptation for some and primarily an act of participation and contribution for others. Attempting to alter these relationships outside of the field without attending to the very real need for those same changes within the field is a mistake. When compositionists use pedagogies that ignore the field, they lose out on opportunities for positive changes within the discipline. That is why the current study focuses on the place of undergraduate students and undergraduate student writing in composition studies. My purpose is to open spaces that will allow us to conceive of participation and contribution as vital activities in the constitution of composition studies for all members of the writing classes, especially those involved in first-year writing courses.

The first chapter discusses and illustrates the importance of using the concepts of participation and contribution to analyze attempts to revise composition studies to open new spaces for student subjectivities. The second chapter looks closely at images of students and teachers embedded within process and post-process discussions of the teaching of writing to illustrate how these images affect four particular attempts at creating spaces for participation and contribution. Chapter three presents an approach to invention, arrangement and revision that simultaneously makes the discourses of the field more important and appropriate material for first-year writing courses, and makes the products of those courses more relevant to composition studies. Chapter four presents a curriculum grounded on the approach presented in chapter three, with particular attention to the issue of faculty development. Chapter five places the work in relation to ongoing discussions about the relationship between theory and practice informing composition studies today. The epilogue discusses very recent work with a new group of faculty who are revising a first-semester writing course in ways that center participation and contribution as vital aspects of critical literacy.

The purpose of this book is to invite teachers of writing, especially teachers of first-year writing, to listen more closely to the ways that undergraduate student writers, their texts, and their teachers are vital to our profession. It is my hope that this work will inspire a commitment to transitions that will open spaces for participation and contribution to all of the members of our writing classes in collaborative and inclusive ways.[4]

1

REVISING PROCESS

For the past 15 years—since early in my graduate school career—I have been struggling to create theoretical, pedagogical, and practical ways to improve the status of undergraduate voices and undergraduate writing in English studies. But in a very real sense, the idea that I could engage in this struggle in ways that mattered grew out of my undergraduate education. It was through undergraduate courses in rhetoric, writing, women's studies, and modern theories of grammar and composition that I became aware that a person could, in fact, pursue goals that were rich and complex in nature, goals that included improving the conditions of life for oneself and others in inter-related ways.

When Dr. Monica Weis, the professor of my undergraduate course in "Modern Theories of Grammar and Composition" invited me to attend the Conference on College Composition and Communication, I was both shocked and deeply honored. After all, I had been less than accepting of some of the theories we studied in that course, especially those that I thought talked down to "non-traditional" students like myself. I was particularly skeptical about expressivist theories like the one I had been subjected to years before when I was a traditional-age student, theories that were quite popular in the late 1980s when I took that theory course. Still, here I was invited by my professor to attend the major conference of the field—with financial support to do so from the college and department that I had clearly thrived in, but which I had never simply identified with. I remember clearly the power of the invitation and the ways in which it made me stretch beyond any kind of thinking I had ever done while trying to figure out what something meant. I also remember the ways in which the invitation made me begin to consider the possibility that there might be a place for me in the world that would continue to stretch my thinking in this way, one where I would not be required to be happy with the way things are in order to belong. It was the first time that I considered the possibility that there might be a way for me to give back as much as I got from my study of writing. It was a rush. I was never very cool before that, but the idea of this possibility squelched any chance I had of being cool—I was on fire. And I have been on fire ever since.

That fire comes from and fuels the desire to participate in and contribute to something rather than merely gain from it. The form it takes in this study is to suggest that revising the prewrite-write-rewrite notion of process that has driven first-year composition in this country in our recent past can enhance structural, curricular, and disciplinary opportunities for participation and contribution. These revisions are theoretical and pedagogical and practical; they are meant to open spaces for a wider range of people to participate in and contribute to composition studies. What happens once these spaces are open will be so informed by the opportunities they will afford us that the arguments I am making here should not be thought of as transformational; they should be understood as transitional. To open the possibilities for transition I am discussing here, I will illustrate and argue for a continuation of recent trends that position analysis rather than mastery as critical to and in composition studies. I will, however, extend the recent focus on analysis in ways that challenge a more general tendency to favor adaptation over contribution and to valorize consumption (especially consumption of first-phase process models) over participation in our configurations of writing in first-year composition classes. In the end, I will suggest that using the concepts of participation and contribution to revise our views of and approaches to composition studies allows us to live up to the promise of the process movement without being bound by its limitations.

While many revised process-based approaches claim transformative power, as suggested above, I am more interested in creating a transitional approach, one that acknowledges first-phase process model assumptions as the starting point for many teachers and students, and that attempts to create ways for us to move together toward literacy practices that center participation and contribution as possibilities for all members of the writing classes. This is especially important in our first-year writing courses where students internalize assumptions about the relationship between language and reality. Making transitions toward practices that change reality in substantial ways is more difficult than identifying methodologies and pedagogies that we think and hope will change individual consciousnesses, but it is also more important. As James Slevin notes, our discipline is used to thinking of professionals as those who participate in and contribute to the field while amateurs/students are positioned as embodying our contributions. Slevin suggests beginning to move away from these assumptions and the realities they create. He states:

> We could, for example, look to the model of the liberal arts college and find there an understanding of disciplinarity that saw teaching and intimate intellectual conversations with students and colleagues at the center of life in that discipline. It would be possible (though let me stress, too, very hard) to imagine this work as primary, with research and publication valuable as they nourish the education of students and extend the collegial conversation to a wider audience. Let me say again that it is hard to think these thoughts—they seem generically pastoral or idyllic, an escapism set against the harsh urbanity and metropolitanism of today's academy. They seem fond wishes rather than empowering conceptual frameworks. (43)

To some of us, those frameworks of and for teaching and learning seem less pastoral and idyllic than the result of commitment and hard work, silenced and undervalued though the work seems to be in the larger scheme of things. How many of us have an understanding of the model Slevin refers to here? How many of us have seen it in actual practice? How valued is that understanding and practice in the larger professional and discursive spaces that constitute the discipline? What takes the place of these absent possibilities in the field?

To say that composition studies should raise students' individual consciousnesses about advertising, or history, or literature, or about academic discourse is not necessarily a bad thing. It is possible, however, to understand consciousness-raising as one of the obstacles to participation and contribution, if consciousness-raising takes the place of participation and contribution, and/or if people are configured as unconscious when they are not, and/or if raised consciousness does nothing to alter the relationships to power made available to those whose consciousness has been raised. The ways these dilemmas about consciousness raising as an end of writing instruction become apparent in composition studies is clear, for example, in the ways that we talk about rather than with our undergraduate students. As Susan Miller notes in *Textual Carnivals*, empirical work about students' texts has long captured the imagination of compositionists (200). In her introduction to *Landmark Essays on Process*, Sondra Perl notes that empirical work about student texts defines one of the most important methodological moves behind the process movement itself. While this methodological approach is one method for increasing how student writing can come into the field, it also blocks student participation in significant ways. For example, student writing can be illustrative, teaching us things about how certain practices affect the process or products produced, but students are not included in the processes of analysis that construct such knowledge from their texts. Positioning students in relation to the discipline in such limiting ways is part of a larger related habit of excluding students from our discussions more generally. The idea that we can change the terms of this material reality by raising and/or empowering individual consciousnesses without challenging these limited notions of literacy in our disciplinary and professional spaces is misinformed. The deferral of the discipline (i.e., perpetuating the idea that thousands of students can take composition classes but can't tell you anything about the disciplinary knowledge of the field) becomes the repression of literate subjectivity (i.e., one can experience and act in the field without ever affecting or engaging in the practices of the discipline). As Kurt Spellmeyer reminds us in "Inventing the University Student," within this scene "nothing could be less helpful . . . than to embrace once again an image of academic intellectuals as representative of 'the people,' 'the silenced,' and so on" (43). This is especially true as we struggle to revise composition studies in ways that open new spaces for student writing and student subjectivities.

This level of revision is never easy. However, exploring student assumptions about the concepts we use, and consider using, to ground our introductory writing courses is something we must do if we want to open new spaces for student subjectivity. Mina Shaughnessey and others took such an exploratory approach toward issues of grammatical correctness and standardization. But few people who are attempting to revise first-year writing courses take engaging students in this part of the endeavor very seriously.[5] Perhaps that is because the work seems too much like drawing a composite or dishonoring the "individual" student writer so entrenched in first-phase process approaches to first-year writing. Or maybe, as Miller indicates, our first-year writing students are so over-constructed as "innocent" literacy vessels that this kind of research just doesn't fit with the program (196). In any case, exploring student assumptions about the concepts we propose making central to the teaching of writing is a fundamental step in finding ways to invite them into our field as participants. Invitations to these activities raise questions about ability, confidence, expectation, and, especially, self/other relationships that many people in the education system are not used to facing together. But this kind of work also indicates very real connections between our concerns with the limitations of first-phase process movement pedagogies and the limitations on literacy assumed by our students.

Before I move to the empirical data that illustrate this point, let me emphasize that breaking through such discursive restrictions is not a new thing for composition teachers and students. For example, many people spent the first phase of the process writing movement trying to create approaches to writing that challenged restrictions regarding what students could write about in our classrooms, and students have, in many cases, embodied this break. One major component of this first phase was the prewrite-write-rewrite model dominating that pedagogical scene of writing. The model centered approaches that allowed students to explore their own experiences, and, in some cases, use "their own voices," to create discourses about subjects that had been considered inappropriate in the past. As many scholars of the field have noted, decentering literary texts in favor of centering student texts, when combined with an emphasis on "authentic" voices and experience, led to the disciplinary construction of a decontextualized student subjectivity (Crowley, DeJoy, Ede, Miller). The primary assumption of the model was that prewriting, writing, and rewriting strategies were constructed, through adaptation of classical rhetoric, secondary and primary research activities, etc., by the scholar/researcher members of the writing class and presented, through textbooks and teachers, as instruction, advice, direction (sometimes heuristic) to the student members of that class. The students were, therefore, invited to talk about unlimited and innumerable subjects, to embody the radical potential of the model, as long as they did so in individualistic ways and as long as knowledge about the disciplinary matters addressed by the profession were not the subject of student discourse. So while at one level, teachers and students were collaborators in breaking the bounds of academic discourse, on another level they were also engaged in a process that maintained the gaps among and between student discourses, teacher discourses, and the professional discourses of composition studies. Students could (and sometimes had to) write about everything from their sex lives and drug use to their dreams and aspirations and everything in between; but they were not, in general, invited to write about the histories, theories, pedagogies, or practices informing their literacy educations or constructing their literacy experiences in writing classrooms.[6] This deferral of disciplinary conversations constituted the major differences between professorial members and student members of the writing class. And it is this deferral that has informed many of the revisions to first phase process movement pedagogies. In "What Is Composition and (if you know what that is) Why Do We Teach It?" David Bartholomae makes this point when he says:

> It is too convenient to say that students, because they are students, do not share in the general problems of writing . . . like writing history or writing literary criticisms, like the problem of the writer's relationship to the discourse that enables his or her writing. (17)[7]

I am not suggesting that revisionist approaches to first phase process movements have discussed this deferral of the discipline as important to their revision activities. What I am suggesting is that we must understand those revisionist critiques in relation to the disciplinary matters that constitute that deferral if we are to create a transitional moment in composition studies. These revisionist pedagogies point to a gap that we have all too often tried to step over as we have attempted to move forward from first phase process models to more social, critical, and/or community-based practices. We have, in some ways, leapt over the discipline in our attempts to put students in relation to the social, to the cultural, to the institutional, to the world. But we must address and be willing to step into this gap, to alter the relationships between and among members of the writing classes, before we can hope to have any effect on the world. Our world cannot be any different if our profession stays the same. The point here is not just that we are part of the world, although that is something to remember. The point is that if we can't do it, we certainly have no right to position students—or anybody else for that matter—as people who must embody such change for us.

This is why I think transition is a better metaphor than transformation as we attempt to deal with the possibilities opened up by revisions to first-phase process movement approaches to composition studies, particularly those theories, pedagogies, and practices aimed at first-year writing. People make transitions; they get transformed. It is, indeed, a particular kind of material error to think of first-year writing as transformational given the structural devaluation of the course, its students, its pedagogies, and its role in material matters like departmental budgets. These devaluations allow first-year writing's active role in the constitution of composition studies to be set aside in the same way that first-phase process model pedagogies allowed the professional and disciplinary matters of the field to be set aside in the classroom. In an odd, but symmetrical way, within this drama the teachers and students of the first-year writing class can be equally disconnected from the discipline. But, first-year writing is best thought of as a place where all members of the writing classes can make transitions that, ideally, are about participation and contribution, rather than a place where all members of the writing classes are transformed. The revisions to process writing that I will discuss here confront this devaluing of first-year writing and the members of its classes in a number of ways if we read them as challenges to these disconnections.

REVISING ANALYSIS

In an earlier article about the work of James Berlin ("Reconfiguring"), I illustrated the ways that he repositions cultural analysis as a major invention activity in first-year writing courses.[8] He accomplishes this by prescribing invention activities that ask students to identify the binary oppositions, cultural codes, and narrative patterns in the texts they read and in their own experiences. In *Rhetorics, Poetics, and Cultures: Refiguring College English Studies*, Berlin outlines the following structure for first-year writing courses:

> The course provides students with a set of heuristics—invention strategies—that grow out of the interaction of rhetoric, structuralism, poststructuralism, semiotics, and cultural studies. . . . In examining any text—print, film, television—students must locate the key terms in the discourse and situate these terms within the structure of meaning of which they form a part. (117)

Locating these key terms occurs when "students first consider the context of the piece, exploring the characteristics of the readership of the [text under consideration] and the historical events surrounding the essay's production, particularly as indicated within the text" (117). Once these terms are located, then, the following process of contextualization occurs. The terms "are first set in relation to their binary opposites as suggested by the text itself . . ." (117). "In [the next] phase, students place these terms within the narrative structural forms suggested by the text, the culturally coded patterns of behavior appropriate for people within certain situations" (118). When students turn to look at their own experiences (as workers, audiences for popular culture media, etc.), they use these same terms to analyze and understand those experiences, thus bridging the gap between the analytic activities constructed through the theories informing the pedagogies and those used by students. In addition, the invention strategies that inform student reading and those that inform student writing are similar in significant ways. There is, of course, still the fact that someone has figured out which strategies will be engaged before the students have even arrived in class, that many approaches have been considered and rejected, while others have been selected, synthesized, and translated into guidelines for practice. But like Richard Ohmann's radical view of the profession, Berlin's pedagogy takes critical understanding rather than mastery of the way things are as the purpose of participating in the writing class.[9] Students are not always already positioned to favor relationships of identification with the texts of the course, or their ideologies of production. Configuring this kind of analysis as key to invention overtly positions something other than adaptation as the process being explored. Clearly, consciousness raising takes a more prominent place than concerns about where the student writing ends up in Berlin's approach. But, bridging the gap between what "real" cultural critics do and what student critics do is a significant revision here, one that gives the course value as an important part of becoming a member of a democratic society who seeks understanding of culture for purposes other than adaptation. Clearly, these revisions are based primarily on introducing invention strategies usually reserved for certain members of the writing classes (theorists) to members not usually thought of as engaging those strategies (undergraduate students, especially first-year undergraduate students in a variety of majors). As my empirical work will show, by the end of high school it is possible that students themselves perceive the use of such critical strategies as inappropriate and/or unexpected. It is possible that the fundamental split between identification of and identification with the terms for making meaning that approaches like Berlin's suggest is foreign to most students by the time they graduate from high school.

James Slevin makes a different but related call for analysis in *Introducing English: Essays in the Intellectual Work of Composition.* Here, Slevin gives the following advice to those who wish to help students "understand and control their writing, and not just adapt to the signifying system we call 'academic discourse'" (193). To reach this goal, Slevin states, students "need to engage fully in its production, to question it, perhaps even to challenge its purpose—in effect, they need to become involved in the kind of analysis that composition scholars and teachers themselves often undertake" (193). This study of academic genres "questions them as well as masters them . . . by both writing within them and contextualizing them" (195). While Slevin proposes that students focus on the history of literacy in America and Berlin proposes that they study a range of texts about a variety of subjects, they agree that students need to analyze and contextualize both the content of their readings and their own related experiences. Consequently, invention activities must position students in ways that prepare them to do something more than merely identify with what they read, study, experience, and write. While Berlin and Slevin are different in many ways, for both revising invention in the writing class is a matter of recovering context. They do not, as Lad Tobin notes of some set of unnamed presenters he heard one year at the "Conference on College Composition and Communication", revise process in relation to content for the purpose of re-imagining content outside of the focus on the personal that Tobin sees at the heart of composition studies. In his introduction to *Taking Stock: The Writing Process Movement in the '90s*, Tobin states:

> If the emphasis on material culture in literary studies is the "comeback of history," then this movement [the critique of process pedagogy] is the "comeback of content." According to this argument, we need to restore real content (in this case Supreme Court cases or advertisements or historical documents and artifacts); to move students away from thinking and writing about their own individual ethnocentric experiences and feelings; to teach the secret tropes and conventions of academic discourse; and to emphasize cultural studies, situatedness, and critique. (6)

Of course, neither Berlin nor Slevin would make the easy distinction between process and content that Tobin asserts here. More importantly, for both Slevin and Berlin, and for many others attempting to revise process, student experiences are deep and significant parts of the picture; experience is, in fact, the thing being contextualized. So, while Tobin does not name what many attempts to revise process are all about in any accurate way, he does articulate what replacing invention activities that center experience *in particular contextualized ways* looks like and feels like for thousands of writing teachers who were and are initiated into the first-phase process movement. As Lisa Ede reminds us later in this same collection, and as many others have noted, the model of process that became popularized was "mechanistic" and "has inevitably oversimplified and distorted a phenomenon whose richness and complexity we have yet adequately to acknowledge" (35). Furthermore, oversimplified versions of writing as a process did not merely create mechanistic pedagogies for student writing. They also created mechanistic approaches to faculty development within which

> Overzealous language arts coordinators and writing program admin-
> istrators . . . assumed that the process approach to teaching could be
> taught in one or two in-service sessions by all those who (including
> myself) forgot that the term "writing process movement" refers not to a
> concrete and material reality but to an ideologically-charged construct.
> (Ede 35)

In other words, thousands of teachers constructed themselves in identification with a version of process that, as it turns out, positioned them in relation to disciplinary matters in the same ways than it positioned students: as embodying practices they did not necessarily understand and that represented watered-down versions of reality, as experiencing and acting out composition studies without necessarily practicing it. In the midst of such critiques of the proposed revisions (e.g. Tobin's) and of the original process movement (e.g. Ede's), how can the hordes of teachers who helped make first-phase process writing the norm in higher education help but feel betrayed?

In other discussions, the call for connecting analysis and invention focuses on strategies used to challenge particular dominant social norms. In "Discourse and Diversity: Experimental Writing Within the Academy," for example, Lillian Bridwell-Bowles discusses the writing activities she has seen challenging "patriarchal discourse practices" (57). She names these alternative practices "toying with academic writing; the risk of challenging conventions; writing without an argument; experiments with form; differences in ways of working" (58). Here, it becomes clear that although knowledge of certain discursive forms (e.g., academic writing and conventions) is part of the picture, it is not the whole picture, and it certainly presents writers as agents who must consider options other than identification with those certain discursive forms as they write. "Finally," as Bridwell-Bowles states, in this context "teaching students to write involves teaching them ways to critique not only their material and their potential readers' needs but also the rhetorical conventions that they are expected to employ in the academy" (43). In a very real sense, Bridwell-Bowles clarifies the need to construct something other than consumption and adaptation as the end of literate activity by including both texts and strategies whose purposes are different.

Like many others, Bridwell-Bowles names this process of revising writing instruction to emphasize something other than consumption and adaptation "critique." The "something other" that this process of critique emphasizes is practice. And, as all of these attempts to revise process indicate, the rhetoric of deliberate action (activism) that comes from the process of critique may spring from and/ or be encoded in texts very different from the textbooks and other materials we institutionalized in first-phase process movements.[10] Krista Ratcliffe's *Anglo-American Feminist Challenges to the Rhetorical Traditions* explores this possibility, as do Miriam Brody's *Manly Writing: Gender, Rhetoric, and the Rise of Composition,* and Mary Daly's *Wickadery.* My own "I Was a Process-Model Baby" takes this approach to revising process, suggesting that the work of feminist writers like Naomi Wolf, bell hooks, Gloria Steinem and others invites us to consider alternatives to the rhetorical invention, arrangement, and revision strategies over-valorized by dominant renditions of the pre-write-write-rewrite model of composing. What we recover in these feminist revisions to the prewrite part of the writing process movement are alternative ways to think about making meaning with language, ways that do not over-valorize *identification with* discourse conventions, even as they acknowledge the importance of being able to do *identification of* those conventions. But to propose such a methodology reintroduces questions about the relationship between writing and reading. The texts that scholars and graduate students are reading become invitations to write in new ways; the translation of those writing practices and/or texts into classroom pedagogies alters the expectations for student writing; and questions about the relationships between what is being read to create those pedagogies and practices, and what can and should be read in the composition classroom reassert themselves in new ways.

There are many more examples of work that revises first-phase process model approaches to composition by proposing, in whole or in part, revisions to the prewriting activities informing dominant first-phase conceptions of writing as process. This is not surprising since, as Sharon Crowley reminds us in "Around 1971: Current-Traditional Rhetoric and Process Models of Composing," invention was the main focus of institutionalizing first-phase writing process movement models (64–74). Ultimately, these revisions challenge not only the specific prewriting activities popularized by those models—freewriting, brainstorming, clustering, etc.—but also the idea that invention activities available to some members of the writing classes should be radically different from those available to other members of the writing classes. Perhaps most importantly, these revisionist pedagogies institute a generative break between identification of and identification with that questions and explores conventions and status-quo assumptions, rather than merely accepting or rejecting them. The professional members of the class recognized these possibilities early on and began weaving analysis of status quo-assumptions about writing and writing instruction as well as personal narrative into the discourse of the profession, the latter in ways not totally incompatible with the ways students were encouraged to use narrative. Critiquing the processes held out as appropriate for the production of student discourses, especially the particular ways they positioned the writing processes of our students as "*the* subject matter for composition studies" is an important stage in acknowledging both the failures of first-phase process movements and their potential (Daiker 2, emphasis mine).

Some of the assumptions about the reading/writing relationship inscribed in such notions of student discourse have made understanding that discourse as contributing to and participating in composition studies a difficult endeavor. People who teach writing, especially those who teach first-year writing—are reading a variety of texts in their roles as teachers and scholars, and those texts are often affecting how they teach writing and their expectations as readers. Although I couldn't have had any idea how much my commitment to understanding the implications of this situation would affect my life and my career, no idea of the possibilities and limitations it would present, it has allowed me to listen to and to learn—especially from students—in ways that always urged me to keep opportunities for others clearly in my range of vision. I still remember the first time I took students in one of my undergraduate writing classes to CCCC, still remember their reactions to the ways presenters talked about undergraduate students. In fact, the ways that all of the students I have invited into our professional forums have reacted to the ways they were discussed there has always helped me to understand how much they had to contribute. It would be impossible to measure the ways that these student readings of our discussions inform my work. It would be equally impossible to measure the affects of revising my first-year writing curriculum to include my students and I in community literacy work. Those discussions have enhanced our abilities to rethink and to practice participation and to make contributions to our communities. Everyone involved remembers the first time one of our GED students passed the exam, the first semester that the writing section of the exam (which used to be the biggest cause of failure for our GED students) became the part of the exam everyone passed. We still remember the first time one of the adult basic education students—a man in his sixties—wrote his name for the first time, and the way that his tutor, Nick, much to our surprise, returned semester after semester to help make this happen. We still remember the first time one of the students in our ESL community literacy class moved up into our GED class. We helped make these things possible, my students and I, by participating as tutors in community literacy classes and by thinking about how what we were studying about composition might allow us to contribute to those classes in productive ways, and to invite others to do the same. We have

written reports for our Project READ partners, worked on recruit-
ment and retention campaigns with them, and done book drives
for their library. In the process of studying and acting, we have bro-
ken through many of the restrictive notions of student discourse in
higher education, not the least of which is that student literacy is
usually a tool for evaluation of students, and, increasingly program
assessment, and not much else. But student expectations that their
literacy work can contribute in these ways is very low at the start of
each semester. The expectation that they might contribute to the
discipline is even lower, as I will discuss in the next section; this is
something to remember as we attempt to create transitions that
invite such activities.

REVISING EXPECTATIONS

There is no doubt that the transition to college writing can be difficult for many students. Understanding the differences between
students' learned assumptions about literacy and the absent possibilities inscribed within those assumptions is important if we want
to see those absent possibilities. As it turns out, understanding student assumptions about literacy is critical to re-imagining student
writing as vital to our profession. While I am not proposing that
my students are representative of the population more generally,
their assumptions about participation and contribution help us
begin to map a course as we attempt to engage in more inclusive
literacy activities than those espoused by dominant institutionalized notions of writing as process.

The data that I am about to present were collected from a set
of placement exams that incoming first-year students wrote in the
fall of 2002. The institution the data come from is a small private
university whose mission is to connect the theoretical and the
practical. It is a school that has always had a strong commitment
to providing education to (mostly) traditional-age students who
need some kind of financial support. At the time of this study, all
incoming students wrote a short timed essay (50 minutes) that
was used to determine which students needed to be in an enhanced first-semester writing course that included more intensive
one-on-one tutoring than did other sections of the course. For the

past few years the English department has been using the following prompt for the placement essay.

> The faculty of our first-year writing program is busy preparing for your arrival, and you can help by writing an essay in which you explain your strengths as a reader and writer. Conclude by stating both what you will contribute to your first-semester Critical Writing, Reading, and Researching class and what you hope to gain from that class.

Six hundred seventeen students took the fall 2002 placement exam. I read each of the essays three times. During the third reading, I created a list of the ways each student discussed what they hoped to gain and what they hoped to contribute to their first-semester class. Because I was most interested in the profile of the group, I created lists of desired gains and contributions, not profiles of individual students. Student consultants I had talked with about this project thought it would be important to code what people hoped to gain as well as what they said they could contribute in case they were hoping to gain opportunities for using literacy to participate in and/or contribute to things like the school newspaper. Not every student who wrote the place-ment exam discussed both participation and contribution, but most made at least some attempt to address these issues in their conclusion as the prompt requested. After I had made these lists, I met with my student assistant, Travis Meisenheimer, to discuss how we might group these responses.[11] We decided that our two major categories—gains and contributions—would be further divided into those most related to writing, those most related to reading, and those most related to researching. After student responses were categorized, Travis and I met with two small focus groups of advanced English majors. All but one of these students had taken the course; one student had transferred from community college and had taken first-year writing there. I wanted to open up inter-pretation of the data from the placement exams to students who could reflect upon the meaning of the responses in a variety of ways. While it is not unusual to use student writing as a database in our field, it is unusual to include students in analysis of that data. But opening up these disciplinary conversations to our students is

critical to our field if we are to expand the possibilities for participation and contribution. I have included fairly lengthy excerpts from our conversations
in this section to illustrate the rich ways that students can help us
to understand the disciplinary matters at issue here. Our conversations took several hours. For the sake of presenting those conversations in relation to issues, I have sometimes rearranged the order
of our comments, especially so that comments about the same
issues from the first and second sessions could be read together.
The student consultants agreed that this would be the best way
to deal with presenting our dialogue, and each read these pages
before any of them have been made public. I invited all students
in the "Internship in the Teaching of Writing" course (a course
required of all of our English Secondary Education majors) and all
of my advisees who had articulated an interest in graduate school
to be in the focus groups; six students agreed to meet for three
one-hour taped sessions to discuss the placement exam data.[12] Our
conversations began with a consideration of the fact that the data
come from placement exams, a particular writing situation that
may reflect much about student expectations for their first semester class and about what they think they are expected to say.

Nicole: I remember when I wrote this essay, and I was thinking that
            I wanted to impress the English professors that would be
            reading it. I remember sitting there that day thinking that,
            maybe they [the students writing the placement exams] felt
            like somebody was going to read it and if they put the wrong
            thing, then they might go into their first class at already
            somewhat of a disadvantage.

Linda: So these essays are kind of layers of expectations. It's what
            the students think is expected of them, what they're expect-
            ed to say.

Carrie: I noticed that too. I thought . . . a lot of these answers are
            what you might put on an application to college . . . even
            though it's just a placement essay, it somehow might matter.

Jennifer: And I almost get the feel from a lot of these that they're
            really struggling to say what they think that you want to
            hear. Almost like it's a job interview; very interesting.

Nancy: In an odd way though, that would show a kind of audience awareness at work, an awareness that isn't articulated as a skill or a strength anywhere in the essays. What you're saying is they have a particular notion of the audience and a particular notion of the purpose of the essay they're writing, and so they're giving these responses, but not putting in the response that audience awareness and knowing what you're "supposed to" say are important. Or, as somebody else said, it's what they think we want to hear which, of course, is telling us a lot about what they think about literacy education, and literacy educators.

Nicole: I think also that . . . in the back of their minds they are thinking I can't come right out and say all I want is an A because then somebody will know that I don't really care about the class.

Jennifer: It seems like a lot of these things [that the students mention] are things that would have been marked on a paper in some way—like especially in a high school classroom—needs more organizational skills, needs more support of argument, or vary your sentence style.

Nancy: Now it's interesting because I hadn't thought of that, and yesterday people said the same thing: that this clearly reflects what they've seen written on their papers.

Linda: This reminds me of all the things I hate about being a student. But you know why they say these things—because this is the expectation. . . . You learn that these are acceptable skills or contributions. . . . These just show you what they expect the priorities to be.

For the student consultants, the essays represent two major writing concerns: a sense that there may be negative consequences for student writers' performances and a concern for meeting audience expectations. The student consultants all assume that the essay writers are bringing past experiences about expectations to bear in their essays. There are many contemporary disciplinary conversations about these matters, both as separate issues and as connected issues. Recall, for example, Peter Elbow's "Closing My Eyes As I Speak: An Argument For Ignoring Audience," or Ede and Lunsford's "Audience Addressed/Audience Invoked: The Role of Audience in Composition Theory and Pedagogy" and the work it draws from (Ong), or Park's "The Meaning of Audience," or the discussion of audience in Bartholomae's "Inventing the University." Consider also the rich historical materials available here: Aristotle's *Rhetoric*, the introduction to Christine dePizan's *Book of the City of Ladies*. We have to start to wonder why these disciplinary discussions and historical texts are not generally seen as content for courses that address students who bring the knowledge and assumptions indicated here with them into our classrooms. We have to start to wonder why we create separate types of discussions about these matters for our students (e.g., rubrics for audience analysis that students are supposed to enact rather than question or explore as particular ways to put writers and readers in relationship with one another). Certainly, student experience in general has not been bracketed from the first-year writing classroom. But the expectation is common that the disciplinary discourses about these concerns will be bracketed, especially in first-year courses.

Another of the more interesting conversations came when one of the student consultants made a connection between the specific context for this writing and the larger educational context behind the scene. As Meg illustrates, at stake here is the possibility that people have internalized limited notions of the ways that writing can create self/other relationships (and/or limited sets of largely mechanical matters that they think ground those relationships). Meg refers here to the fact that very few students talked about their written language as being able to contribute to the class, but that many defined their contributions in relationship to their oral literacy (talking in class) and to working hard.

Meg: Maybe students—by the time they've graduated from high school—perceive their contributions primarily in this way. That they can say something in class, they can participate in the discussion, but their idea of being able to contribute in any other way—maybe there's so many of those because it's the one way people feel like they can contribute—they say that because they don't have anything else to say. The idea that their reading or writing might contribute to class is, for whatever reason, like Kathy was saying before, about how they just expect to read something and come in and repeat what it said rather than do something else with it. They don't see that as contributions. They may see it as some type of performance, but they don't see it as contributions.

Nancy: So, why is it that working hard and having opinions are considered primary and safe ways to think about contribution?

Jennifer: It implies on some level that you care about the course. Having an opinion is the same thing. Even if the work you are doing isn't of high quality, but you're doing something—if you're writing something, or just fixing grammatical errors . . .

Linda: Everybody's told them they'll have to work hard. And it sounds good.

Nancy: Well, it does sound good to say you're going to work hard. But, think about it this way for a minute. What if those are just the default things that these students say? Like they get to the part where they're supposed to talk about the things they can contribute, and they don't know what to say. So the default mode is to say that you'll work hard and express your opinion in class.

Jennifer: It doesn't imply any kind of progress or insight. You just have to be there and talk and do something. It doesn't matter what you do or what you say as long as you're functioning on some level as a student of the class.

Linda: Yes, [talking in class and working hard] sound like default answers, what they think teachers want to hear. Of course, work hard, and if you have an opinion you're going to speak up in class.

Nancy: What else do you think? There's a section here where people talked about product-centered contributions. Only 24 people said that their actual writing—like their papers— were going to be part of what they actually contributed to the course. Only 24 people said that their actual papers would be something they were contributing. That is the thing that shocked me the most.

Jennifer: I think that says something about the way these students perceive their own ability as writers in a writing class, if they don't think they are contributing their own writing on some level.

Linda: I'm still trying to picture what I would say. I don't think that people would say stuff like " I'm going to contribute my fantastic writing" because it doesn't sound very humble. You don't know anything—you're a student. That's why you're a student. It's almost an unfair question. What are you going to contribute as somebody whose been trained for years that you're not a contributor. You're an empty vessel to be filled.

Jennifer: Well, like Linda said, to assert something like that [that student papers could contribute to a course of study] would be an act of self-empowerment almost. Like this is something that I did, and it's important and I'm contributing with it. Not to say that implies a lot of distance between yourself and the product. [But this] conception of literacy has gotten them this far.

Kathy: Going back to knowledge, I kind of got the feeling they thought knowledge was—they expressed knowledge as the action of doing the writing instead of what they generated . . .

Nancy: I hadn't put those two things together until you said that.

Kathy: It felt like they viewed knowledge as . . . skills.

Jennifer: But [their responses are] not [about] the process of writing either, it's the end result—grammatically correct and organized well, etc.

Meg: I think they think they are writing just for teachers, so why would [their writing] ever contribute to other students?

Carrie: They're just creating to get a good grade.

Linda: And, of course, if all you get from reading is comprehension, then all you need from writing is to show that you understood [what you read].

Jennifer: Along with that, it's interesting to me, there's nothing about challenging the research [you are presented with].

Nancy: No, there's nothing about adding to it or challenging it. Although analyzing could mean that you say some is good research and some isn't. Again, mostly about skills.

Jennifer: And knowledge of the system. These all seem very removed from the student, too . . . it's all part of the process of getting this thing done in a certain way. It's not involved. There's no questioning or challenging.

Nancy: The way that it's supposed to be is already set. And what you're doing is trying to figure out how to get there. That came up yesterday a lot too. Like Meg said at one point, "I just wish I could hug all these poor children. I think they're in a lot of pain."

We could see that student writers are often more worried about meeting the expectations of an audience who will evaluate their work than they are about the relationship between their work and the discipline as a larger context within which it might have meaning. As student consultants noted, this conceptualization of audience valorizes comprehension and repetition as the end of composition. The data also present us with a way to understand the connections between, on the one hand, that concern and a focus on mechanical and organizational matters and, on the other hand, a generalized conception of knowledge as skill in relation to writing. I asked student consultants to consider the definition of writing implied by our data.

Nancy: If you had just this data, if somebody said, "Here's some information. From this construct a definition of writing."

Jennifer: I think for the most part, ideal writing would be cohesive, grammatically correct, organized well. It's not really about the content itself.

Nancy: Here we have a group of people who have been getting some sort of literacy education since they were at least 5. How is it possible that people who have been practicing something this long—now think about it, say it was the piano and you had been practicing for 15 years – and not expect to be pretty good at it?

Linda: No, not if you started at lesson 1 every year. Because that's that whole blank slate thing. You walk in with the expectation that you have to do whatever that particular instructor wants, and they assume you know nothing at all, so you start over and over and over and over. So there is no getting better.

Nancy: Do you think students spend at least as much time trying to figure out [what the teacher wants] as they do learning things about writing and reading?

Jennifer: I think they spend more time with that.

Linda: Yes, because the real point of each course is what you have to do to survive.

Jennifer: It just kind of turns you into a grade collector at some level. And then once you have this perfect formula of exactly how much you have to do and what way you do it to achieve your desired level of progress or evaluation, then you're set. There's this removal from the content.

Perhaps this explains, at least in part, why there were only 24 responses about the ways student writing could be seen as a contribution in any way, when 617 students discussed what they hoped to contribute to their first semester Critical Writing, Reading, and Research course. Furthermore, the responses indicate that even those few people who see their writing as contributing to the course at all do so primarily in relation to undefined issues of quality. Here are all of the contributions that the incoming students were able to imagine:

Writing Contributions

Good papers
Good papers
Good essays
Good essays
Good research papers and essays
Good papers
Some good writing
Thoughtful pieces
Produce quality research
Best work (writing)
Work I can be proud of
Make my writing stand out
A lot of writing
Good writing skills
Write with power
Well-written essays
My writing
Many writing styles
Expressive writing
A lot of emotion in my papers

Balance of humor and seriousness in my work
Unique writing style
Read my own papers thoroughly and correct them
Contribute a little in finding out what I want to write about

But as my student consultants predicted, when we combine this set of responses with what students said they hope to gain as writers in the class, an interesting picture emerges, one that helps us to understand what students think they need to become better writers. What is most striking, even if not surprising, is that although there were only 24 responses about student writing possibly counting as a course contribution, there are 653 responses regarding what students hope to gain as writers (obviously, some of the 617 students said more than one thing about what they hoped to gain as writers).

Writing Gains

Improve mechanics (grammar, spelling, punctuation)	44
Improve writing skills (unspecified)	44
Become better at process of putting things down on paper	36
Become a better writer (unspecified)	30
Improve structure/organization	29
Improve quality of my writing	27
Improve expressive abilities	26
Better knowledge of writing	22
Improve/expand ability to write in different styles	21
Improve vocabulary	19
Improve clarity	14
Improve ability to communicate in writing	11
Improve focus in writing	10
Learn to write for college	11
Gain confidence as a writer	12
Gain experience as a writer	9
Improve conclusions	8
Like writing more	9
Improve introductions	6
Improve writing techniques	5
Opportunity to write about a topic of interest	6

Improve research writing skills	6
Improve creativity	5
Make writing easier	3
Gain experience as a peer editor	2
Miscellaneous	24
Total	*439*

In addition to these more specific gains, 107 students also articulated a general desire to improve on their strengths and weaknesses as readers and writers, 81 expressed a desire to improve reading and writing skills, 26 expressed a desire to improve reading, writing, and research skills and/or products. These general comments reflect students' tendency to conclude their essays with a general statement about what they hope to gain across the categories they were asked to discuss in the essay. In any case, these responses indicate that student expectations for writing classes still revolve around current-traditional notions of the importance of surface structures and correctness. They also reflect only a fraction of what one might hope to gain as a writer in a writing class and, as student consultants propose, it may be that this image of themselves as writers is a representation of how they have been taught to act as writers.

Obviously, many of the alternatives to invention, like Berlin's, set purposes for composition instruction—consciousness raising and participation in civic discourse, for example—that challenge the conception of writing and writing courses indicated by these data. But the idea that analyzing invention strategies and discourse more generally—rather than adherence to the prewriting activities and forms of "student" discourse prescribed by first-phase process teachers and textbooks—raises questions about what is to be analyzed as well as how it is to be analyzed. It also raises questions about positioning others in the restrictive ways that oversimplification of writing issues positioned us. Most pointedly, the dominant notion of process positioned reading materials as incapable of giving us information about process. Donald Murray was one of the biggest proponents of this view of reading.[13] As my student consultants and I noticed, this conceptualization of reading fits students' expectations about the role of reading in their literacy lives in significant ways; that is, in both scenarios, the professional and the empirical, you can't learn much about writing from reading. Since these assumptions about the reading/writing relationship are reflected in our data, I move now to a discussion of that data.

Reading Contributions

Interpretation skills	16
Good reading skills	11
Help others understanding materials	9
Reading comprehension skills	8
Reading skills taught in high school	3
Help others love reading	3
Work hard at understanding readings so I can give good ideas/opinions	3
Quick understanding and observation	1
Understanding, knowledge, abilities	1
Wisdom	1
Information	1
Exciting facts	1
Total	56

Desired Reading Gains

Better Reading and Writing skills	81
Improve comprehension	36
Improve knowledge of literature	27
Improve reading, writing, and research	26
Improve speed/read faster	23
Improve reading skills	23
Enjoy reading more	18
Read faster and improve comprehension	17
Exposure to new readings	16
Improve analysis/interpretation skills	15
Miscellaneous	7
Slow down while reading	4
Total	293

One hundred ninety students said that they would contribute ideas and opinions in class (64 said ideas, good ideas, or original ideas; 73 said my opinion/point of view or unique opinions and views; 53 said participation in class discussions). We also noticed that while many students cited a form of speaking in class as a way to contribute, only 8 students said that being a good listener would count as a form of contribution.[14] I asked student consultants to begin by considering the definition of literacy at work in the data about reading contributions and gains.

Nancy: So, thinking about all this together—the gains and contributions part [of the section about reading]—I'm going to ask again—this is a hard question—what do these people think literacy is? If you had to draw an operational definition of literacy from this information, what would you say literacy is?

Linda: The ability to read and comprehend other people's ideas and reorganize them and put them on paper and prove that you comprehended them.

Jennifer: And it really doesn't go beyond that: comprehending, reading, being able to write cohesively and grammatically and having something to say. It doesn't imply anything about applying or challenging it [what you read].

Nancy: And there's a lot about reading faster and understanding more. That is one of the biggest categories here.

Linda: I think that reflects the prior speculation about what we read for—to comprehend what somebody else says or thinks and write to show that you comprehend it.

Nancy: But the writing gains aren't about showing that you understood what you read as much as they are about mechanics, style, and organization.

Linda: What they don't say is, again, anything about content.

Jennifer: So their definition of writing doesn't concern the content at all. It's just the art of being able to write for the assignment. It seems like reading and writing are two very separate things for them. And they really don't consider themselves very good readers or writers.

Nancy: Even though they've been doing it for a long time. This idea that reading and writing seem to be separate things for them came up in yesterday's session too. People were saying that seemed really weird. They don't think they can learn anything about how to write from reading and they don't think they can learn anything about how to read from writing.

Jennifer: It seems like the expectations placed on them for reading and writing are very different. There's attention to grammar and to structure and to all of these mechanical surface things with writing, but with reading it's more comprehension and identification. There isn't really like a personal level with either of them, but they're different. And neither of those sets of expectations really gets to the . . . I think they're still very distant and kind of stop at comprehension. It seems like they do reading as a means to an end. It's like something that you have to defeat or conquer. It's not a process of learning. You have to demolish the book. I'm going to read it faster and more efficient[ly]. I'm going to dominate it, and that's going to be it. And it's not even about personal growth or anything. . . . But knowing what you have to know.

Nancy: Nobody says I want to use reading to become a better person, or to help me understand the world more, or whatever.

Jennifer: Or [be] a better writer.

Travis: Of course not—everything's segmented.

Nancy: That's becoming more and more of a theme here—everything's segmented out.

Travis: Reading and writing don't mix.

Jennifer: And the ways you go about becoming a better writer are completely different than the ways you go about becoming a better reader.

But revisions to first-phase process that open the conversation about student/discipline relationships make no such assumption. In fact, revised approaches to composition assert that a variety of kinds of knowledge can be gained both from reading things other than student papers in writing classes and from reading student papers in new ways. What's more, revised approaches that create an important place for analysis in invention also discuss inclusion as a textual matter. According to Slevin, we can learn about the history of literacy in America and about how that history positions literate subjectivity in ways that call for multiple responses such as resistance, adherence, and rejection in relation to our own experiences. According to Berlin, we can learn about and decode status-quo cultural assumptions and personal experience by analyzing a variety of texts from popular culture. According to Bridwell-Bowles, we can learn about how to generate "more critical readings of patriarchal discourse practices" by reading feminist texts. This list could go on and on. The point here is that those who have revised the writing process movement have struggled to connect reading and writing in ways that acknowledge and enact both the generative and the analytic possibilities of literate rhetorical action.[15] In doing so, they emphasize the fact that arrangement is never merely about the order of words and sentences and paragraphs on a page; arrangement is always also about the relationships referred to and implied by texts, and, therefore, about the world. This is a very different struggle than those favored by textbooks that defer the question of reading—even readings of themselves—in favor of presenting instructional materials that it is assumed students will identify with—or at least pretend to—in order to succeed. Analysis—or at least the kinds of analysis engaged by people who are serious about revising process—proposes ways of reading and writing that break the cycle of identification of/identification with often assumed in literacy studies. Comprehension is not restricted to learning only about the text, and what it helps us learn about is not expected to generate simple identifications. In a very real sense, the idea that texts can be used to forward the inclusion of new methods of analysis opens both the materials and the methods of composition studies to critique, even to student critique, as anyone who has tried such an approach will tell you. That these revisions have occurred primarily without simultaneous attention to the matters of participation and contribution means, I believe that, despite the possibilities they open, they are always in danger of merely calling up the same "student writer," whose writing and subjectivity are restricted to embodying and consuming rather than participating in and contributing to composition studies. This is why I am calling for further revisions, revisions that make participation and contribution central to composition studies.

REVISING STUDENT SUBJECTIVITY

Whereas first-phase models of process positioned the rewriting of student texts as the locus for revision, revisions to process tend to center some aspect of student subjectivity as the thing being revised through composition studies. The writing might be intransitive, but the consciousness it comes from and affects is not. For example, Berlin's goal is to change student consciousness, Bridwell-Bowles would like to change the relationship between student writers and their experiences as writers, Slevin wants to revise students' relationships to what he constructs as disciplinary knowledge and action, and so on. In each case, something other than merely a student product is being revised, usually not for the primary purpose of adapting to traditional standards for student prose, but for the purpose of inviting some form of critical consciousness and/or critique. This is not to say that first-phase approaches did not attempt to—and in some cases succeed in—revising theory, pedagogy, and practice. The point is that they did not apply the same notion of revision to their instructional materials for students; there, revision was—and still is—primarily restricted to rewriting and to whatever textual matters need to be addressed as students move toward the final version of a product (see the essays in *Crisis and Change* for a variety of discussions about this matter). One of the major differences between first-phase models of writing as process and current revisions to those models is that in the first-phase approaches prewriting, writing, and rewriting are matters of production and are assumed to be universally applicable in any writing situation and for any purpose, while attempts to revise these approaches recognize the ways that prescribed notions of production are ideologically particular. In fact, like many contemporary methods of critique, those employed by people attempting to change the theories, pedagogies, and practices of first-phase process movement assumptions in revisionary ways are not only engaged in revision activities. They are configuring revision as central to composition studies—both in relation to student subjectivity and to English studies more generally—in ways that are radically different from the revision practices that define student writing in first-phase notions of process writing. Bartholomae presents a particular case in point in "What Is Composition and (if you know what that is) Why Do We Teach It?" He states:

> [Composition] is . . . a way of committing professional time and energy to the revision of the [student] essay—both as it is the product of institutional goals and practices (composition, then, is a commitment to study, critique and change writing in the schools) and as the product of a particular writing at a particular point in time (composition, then, is a commitment to intervene in and direct the practices of individual writers). Composition would take its work to be revision; the form of composition I am willing to teach would direct the revision of the [student] essay as an exercise in criticism (even, I think I would say, cultural criticism—that is I would want students not only to question the force of the text but also the way the text positions them in relationship to the history of writing).
>
> This binds composition to the ordinary in ways that are professionally difficult. It takes as its subject the [student] essay rather than Toulmin, and this buys less in the academic marketplace. And it ends with revisions that are small, local, and difficult to value. It assumes the direct intervention in specific projects where (from a certain angle of vision) the gains are small. (21)

Bartholomae's process of revision revolves around the reading of other texts (in this essay Mary Louise Pratt's *Imperial Eyes*) and teacher "intervention." Despite the fact that the role of reading texts other-than-student texts is not discussed as part of this program for composition studies, reimagining the role of reading in composition does constitute a major ground for revising process. Unlike Bartholomae, I do not believe that we can or should maintain an either/or binary between the texts of our discipline and student discourses, especially the student discourses of first-year writing class students. The assumption that revisions related to student writing must be "small, local, and difficult to value" sets aside the possibility that students and student discourses can and do participate in and contribute to composition studies. In many ways, these assumptions imply what I will make overt: revising composition studies in ways that make the promises of first-phase process movements a reality requires us to explore the absent possibility of student participation and contribution in relation to a variety of disciplinary matters, including the dominant prewrite/write/rewrite paradigm valorized by those movements. That paradigm centered a process/product binary that re-covered the possibility of challenging the ideology of consumption/adaptation, thereby re-inscribing limited—and limiting—roles for student writing in composition studies.

2

REVISING (RE)VISIONS

In this chapter I will examine the ways that two images of students and teachers operate to restrict the agency of many members of writing classes in composition studies. I will then analyze the ways that some specific challenges to these images open and close spaces for participation and contribution to become features of the discipline. Analysis of these revisions illustrates the ways that struggling to create theoretical and pedagogical openings for participation and contribution challenge more conventional narratives of teachers and students that have informed images of first-year writers and their teachers. In the end, even these revised spaces are interrupted by a configuration of the discipline as closed to undergraduate student participation and contribution. Nevertheless, a close view of the ways that revised approaches imagine new relationships between writers and the world offers valuable insight into how we might alter the relationships between and among writing students, teachers and the discipline.

IMAGES OF STUDENTS AND TEACHERS IN (POST)PROCESS

In *Writing Students: Composition Testimonials and Representations of Students*, Marguerite H. Helmers makes three crucial observations about the ways students are represented in testimonials about composition teaching:

1. "Within the testimonial is the stock figure of *the student*, a character whose inability to perform well in school is his defining feature" (4).
2. "Students have been the subject of despair, ridicule, rhetorical distancing, and fear for centuries. Rabelais' Gargantua was not only a giant, but also a slow and dimwitted student who took five years and three months to memorize his ABCs and another thirteen years, six months, and two weeks to learn grammar and courtesy (Rabelais 38)" (5).

3. "[Student] writing comes to represent a person, a set of traits ascribed to an individual." (5)

The students are what they write, and moreover, they mark themselves by their unstable writing as something Other than the professionals whose texts are revered in academe. As Miller writes in *Rescuing the Subject*, "'many theorists and teachers of written composition still unquestioningly emphasize a direct connection between thought and spoken-to-written language' while also lamenting 'the differences between 'authors' and the halting textual voices of imitative . . . student writing'" (9–10).

As Helmers notes, revising this view of students is more complicated than merely saying we will now think of students as writers. Instead, "practitioners and writers need to envision in new ways the relationships and underlying assumptions of the field to reverse hierarchies and replace [these] familiar representations" (17). By positioning this new vision at the center of composition studies, Helmers's work represents and suggests the fundamental challenges faced by people who have taken revision of first-phase process movements as their goal. Both the testimonial lore about students that informs the construction of composition as a discipline and the hierarchies that have informed the composition classroom are challenged by many late twentieth-century attempts to revise first-phase process movements. Most significantly, Helmers predicts that these revisions must be constructed, negotiated, and enacted not only by professionals in the field, but also by the practitioners and writers who constitute its population.

Although many scholars within composition studies have recognized that the need for more participation-based approaches to revisioning composition studies has been growing, we have had some difficulty constituting the ground of this shared work. As I will illustrate through analyzing some of these revisions to first-phase models, that difficulty is inscribed through theoretical and pedagogical strategies that repress and defer the discipline of composition studies at the level of practice. Later in this chapter, I will illustrate how some of these revisionary pedagogical movements create grounds for transitions that begin to make participation and contribution central to composition studies. Before moving to analyze those specific revisions, however, I would like to outline and challenge another narrative structure they interrupt, one that has been imposed by the more recent construction of a "post-process" paradigm. Although this scene of writing inscribes a different narrative structure than the one that Helmers identifies, it expands the cooptation of agency she identifies as informing earlier movements. In the end, I will illustrate that we must create a very different narrative if we want to do the kinds of analysis, theorizing, and pedagogy building that help us make transitions toward more inclusive practices.

The post-process narrative of students and teachers that I am referring to here emerges fairly early in attempts to separate post-process/social-turn theories and pedagogies from writing process pedagogies. In one of the earliest versions of this narrative, John Trimbur's 1994 rendition, the cooptation of student agency inscribed in the narrative Helmers identifies is expanded to include teachers. To be clear, I do not disagree with much of what Trimbur says in this article and in other places. But the story he tells of process pedagogy—a story that ends by centralizing theory—oversimplifies the process classroom in many ways, failing to acknowledge that many of us who teach two to four sections of first-year writing per year had very different responses to the problems he identifies than the response he narrates. The story he tells restricts the agency of the actors in the scene of composition studies as strongly as does the narrative identified by Helmers. In fact, this story of the process movement and classroom "seems to be on its way to constructing its own narrative of transformation with process as the necessary caricature" (Matsuda 74). This caricature, according to Matsuda, is the result of using the term "post-process" in a particular way, the way Thomas Kent applies it: "as a way of solidifying disparate critiques of so-called expressivism and cognitive theories and pedagogies" (74). As Trimbur illustrates, within these post-process critiques a particular version of the failure of process emerges.

In his review, Trimbur speculates that Patricia Bizzell's *Academic Discourse and Critical Consciousness*, C. H. Knoblauch and Lil Brannon's *Critical Teaching and the Idea of Literacy*, and Kurt Spellmeyer's *Common Ground: Dialogue, Understanding, and the Teaching of Composition* can be read as emerging from "a crisis within the process paradigm and a growing disillusion with its limits and pressures" (109). Trimbur goes on to note that at the center of this "crisis" is the fact that

> the distinction between product and process, which initially seemed so clarifying, not only proved conceptually inadequate to what writers do when they are writing, it also made writing instruction appear to be easier than it is. (109)

Before beginning his review Trimbur states his purpose: "My aim in this review is to note how Knoblauch and Brannon, Spellmeyer, and Bizzell have dealt with this crisis in the process movement and, in particular, how they have figured the problem of the teacher's authority in the writing classroom" (110). To meet this purpose Trimbur presents the following snapshots of the process classroom teacher and student. It is important to quote these descriptions at some length.

> By defining the teacher's role as that of facilitator or co-learner or collaborator, process teachers attempted to relinquish authority unproblematically, in order to empower the expressive capabilities of their students. These teachers, however, ran into some very real problems. For one thing, students often reinscribed the authority that process teachers were trying to vacate, for the very simple reason that they knew their composing processes would eventually result in a product for evaluation, and the canniest among them recognized that sincerity and authenticity of voice were the privileged means of symbolic exchange. In an interesting inversion, at least some of the students in process classrooms proved to be better rhetoricians than their teachers. . . . If process teachers were reading what they took to be direct and unmediated prose of personal experience, the most successful students were hard at work constructing the authorial persona of self-revelatory personal essays written in a decidedly non-academic style. To put it another way, the irony of process pedagogy is that teachers' desire to operate outside oppressive institutions and avoid the errors of the past only reinstituted the rhetoric of the belletristic tradition at the center of the writing classroom. (110)

In this scene, teachers are naïve caretakers with good intentions who have neglected the responsibilities of their authority. As a result, students are not defined by lacks and absences, as they have been in the past, but by their ability to play the game better than their writing teachers. Teachers however, are simultaneously defined by lacks and absences—a lack of authority and an absence of understanding, at least. In this scene, everyone has been duped (and the "canniest" and "more sophisticated students" have become dupers). What is important to note here, is that the post-process/ social turn movement positions theorizing as the new ground of and for composition studies, as the missing link, as what the process movement lacks. Trimbur states: "My point . . . is what appeared to be so clarifying and liberating was inevitably caught in a dense and overdetermined web of textual realities and rhetorical relationships that process pedagogy had failed to theorize" (110).[16]

Like the narrative Helmers presents, this story ends with restricted notions of agency. You will recall that the narrative Helmers identifies ends with the cooptation of student agency and the over-valorization of the instructor's agency. In Trimbur's version of the social turn narrative agency has been abandoned altogether; it is "process pedagogy" that has failed to theorize what needed to be theorized. This, of course, paves the way for theory—and theorists—to take center stage as agents of the field.[17] A new narrative pattern for responding to the challenges of teaching writing emerges here: The theorist perceives a lack or absence in a pedagogy, the theorist constructs a picture of the whole pedagogical scene based on that lack or absence, the theorist interprets old and new practices in relation to that lack or absence. This is a particular notion of theory—and theorizing. More importantly, however, if theory is to be given this kind of power in this way, then whether we work to give everyone access to that power or create/ save such power for a few elite members of the writing classes is the decision we face.

ALTERNATIVE REFLECTIONS

What Trimbur's story covers over are all of the alternative responses to "reinstitut[ing] . . . the belletristic at the center of

the writing classroom" that have emerged from process classrooms. I have heard many stories about responding to these
process classroom challenges in very different ways from those
narrated by Trimbur (at workshops across the country, from colleagues at other institutions, and at my home institution where
two colleagues and I have developed an alternative that works in
our context (more about this in later chapters)). We were not
taken back—to the belletristic tradition or backward more generally—by the real problems of process pedagogy. This is because
many people who teach first-year writing, including myself, never
believed that process pedagogy was a rule to be followed, but was
a complex approach to the teaching of writing that required not
mere adoption, but critique and revision at the level of practice.
Many of us, that is, did not construct our pedagogies only in
identification with process pedagogy. Our relationships to that
movement—as students and as teachers—were and are more
complex and institutionally specific than that. For many people
the process movement marked a serious change in our relationships with models for teaching first-year writing, opening up not
only the issues Trimbur claims for social-turn theories, but also
encouraging responses that repositioned students as critical participants in the discipline.[18] In fact, I would argue that Trimbur's
version of the story more accurately represents the problems
faced by teachers in programs that prescribe a particular process approach when that approach has been constructed without them. But I would not blame a lack of theorizing for those
problems. Instead, I would trace these problems to the following
three conditions: first, programmatic approaches that prescribe
pedagogies rather than creating collaborative forums for program and faculty development; second, institutional exploitation
of writing teachers; third, a growing conservatism in the professional and disciplinary structures that devalues first-year writing
and its teachers and students. The perceived lack of theorizing
about, and more generally responding to, these issues by practitioners who experience problems in the classroom is most
likely a result of publishing practices that favor certain types of

discourse, and/or of the fact that teaching in graduate programs is so overvalued as the immediate end of graduate education in our field than a result of a lack of theorizing and revision on the part of undergraduate teachers. Covering over these material realities creates and maintains a traditional notion of disciplinarity in composition studies. My point is that there is another way to write this story of how we deal with the potential and challenges of the first-phase process movement and its pedagogies, one that centers participation and contribution as vital to composition studies, one that some of us have been writing for a long time. Imagine this alternative story:[19]

> *By defining teachers as facilitators or co-learners or collaborators, process teachers attempted to empower the expressive capabilities of their students and their own pedagogical positions. They ran into some very real challenges. Most important, they noticed that their students were much more capable rhetoricians than they had imagined them to be. Students could, for example, recognize and enact privileged means of symbolic exchange. They could identify and meet audience expectations even when those expectations were covered over by pedagogical methods, and they could master a genre that even their teachers had failed to realize they were calling into existence. To put it another way, the advantage of process pedagogy was that it helped everyone in composition studies to see that students were capable of participating in and contributing to the field in vital and revealing ways. It challenged the teacher/learner binary that has been at the center of higher education for so long. My point, then, is that what appeared to be a pedagogical method to be consumed by teachers and students became the movement upon which members of writing classes could ground more egalitarian practices, pedagogies, and constructions of the field of composition studies itself. Clearly, revisions would be necessary to make this happen. And there was no doubt that it would take time to create material realities that could accommodate participatory roles for teachers and students who had been so strongly constructed as consumers for so long. Failed attempts were inevitable. But the process approach had at least opened the possibility that composition studies could challenge and overcome the mistaken assumptions about students and teachers upon which it had constructed a restricted and restricting notion of their literate abilities. It made clear that resistance to old patterns was necessary for understanding the potential of the field.*

In this alternative to the story that post-process/social turn critiques narrate, the fact that students realize, understand, and can practice the rhetorics they are presented with in composition classes is the ground upon which the field revisions its assumptions and potential. This is the ground upon which we can move toward composition pedagogies that assume all members of writing classes to be capable of more than consumption and reproduction. Slowing down to look at the ground constituted by these revised approaches to process, and reading them for the purpose of honoring the very deep and real ways that they struggle to write a story of composition studies that integrates the analytic and generative possibilities of literacy, is vital if we want to revision the discipline. Key figures in our field have already begun to give us ways to read these possibilities. Here, I will look at examples from five such figures in our field: James A. Berlin, Nora Bacon, Bruce Herzberg, Linda Flower, and Bruce McComiskey. Specifically, I will look at the move from mastery to analysis in the later work of James A. Berlin (1988–1994), a selection of essays from *Writing the Community: Concepts and Models for Service –Learning in Composition* (1997), edited by Linda Adler-Kassner, Robert Crooks, and Ann Watters, and Bruce McComiskey's *Teaching Composition as a Social Process* (2000). It is no surprise that the work under discussion here fails to fit into either the process or post-process configuration of the field. Those who work to create different spaces for student subjectivity are worried about a different set of pedagogical, theoretical, and practical issues.

It is not my intention to summarize these approaches. My goal, instead, is to identify strategies and potential obstacles we face in constructing participation and contribution as critical to composition studies. The theories and pedagogies I will discuss here interrupt both the narrative structures identified by Helmers and the one constructed by Trimbur. I have chosen these specific cases for two reasons. First, because each resists total re-inscription of these narratives, each helps us see the transition toward more participation-based approaches to composition studies. Second, we can better develop a new view of the field if we explore how these approaches pave the way for centering participation and contribution.

REDEFINING THE TERMS OF/FOR COMPOSITION STUDIES
THROUGH THE WORK OF JAMES A. BERLIN

Many people remember and discuss Berlin's work in the history of writing instruction in America. Here, however, I will focus primarily on a critical move in his construction of a pedagogy that began to position participation as the ground of/for composition studies. Berlin was my major professor while I was in graduate school at Purdue University, and I gained much from his generosities as a teacher and learner who did not require approval or reproduction of his own assumptions as the end of his interactions with students. In many ways Berlin's influence was a paradigm for a different kind of relationship between teachers and learners, one in which a traditional notion of identification was neither required nor preferred in the constitution of successful dialogue. I invoke his work here not because I studied with him, however. In fact, we were not always in agreement about how to revise the construction of literacy behind composition studies, even though we agreed that doing so was critical to inviting members of the writing classes into participatory rather than merely reproductive positions. Rather, I read his work as one of the most effective ways to create transitions toward that goal. I will focus here on the methodological move that most strongly supports this critical invitation: the move from mastery to analysis. The methodological move away from assuming mastery to constituting analysis as the ground of/for composition studies in Berlin's work can be understood through his discussions of the rhetoric of the rhetorical situation. In *Writing Instruction in Nineteenth Century American Colleges and Universities,* for example, Berlin begins by extending an idea he first introduced in "Current-Traditional Rhetoric: Paradigm and Practice," an article coauthored with Robert Inkster in 1980.

> Rhetoric has traditionally been seen as based on four elements interacting with each other: reality, writer or speaker, audience, and language. Rhetorical schemes differ from each other, I am convinced, not in emphasizing one of these elements over another. Rhetorical schemes differ in the way that each element is defined, as well as in the conception of the relation of the elements to each other. (1–2)

Here, Berlin illustrates that redefining the elements and relationships of rhetorical situatedness itself is a key step in revising pedagogy. By 1988, in "Rhetoric and Ideology In the Writing Class," Berlin has renamed the referents for all of the traditional exigencies of rhetorical situatedness, calling them "the observer, the discourse community in which the observer is functioning, and the material conditions of existence" (458). Furthermore, he has redefined each of these terms in relation to theories of class and post-structuralist theories of language. One can see his work for details about these redefinitions. What is of interest here, however, is that instead of treating rhetorical situatedness as a tool for adaptation, throughout his work Berlin moves progressively toward a notion of rhetorical situatedness as a tool for analysis not applied for adaptive purposes. This may seem like a minor point. But in the story of revising composition studies in ways that invite participation, it is a significant event: In this scenario, identification of the terms for literacy does not necessarily require identification with those terms, and, in fact, positions critique rather than identification as the practice of first semester writing courses. Both the analytic and generative possibilities of literate activity open out beyond identification of and with the readings and practices that constitute course materials. As I discussed in the first chapter, Berlin enacted these possibilities by closing the gap between the analytic tools used by the theorists he engages to create the pedagogy and those used by students. In addition, these tools are engaged pedagogically not only to analyze the texts of the writing class, but also as generative heuristics in students' processes of production. For me, this is one of the most significant movements of late twentieth century revisions to first-phase process movements. However, the pedagogy pre-constructs those tools from theories and texts that the students and teachers rarely look at together, maintaining a gap between the texts that constitute some of the spaces of composition studies (the theoretical and the professional, for example) and those that constitute other spaces of composition studies (the classroom and student texts, for example), maintaining the traditional hierarchies of the field. But the pedagogy also begins to "resist the hierarchy of specialization that has separated the teaching of writing from the teaching of reading," (*Rhetorics, Poetics, Cultures* 115), the major tenet of first-phase process model movements' dominant practices. In addition, the fact that the pedagogy repositions the relationship between reading and writing as central to process pedagogy in ways that still allow for familiar practices such as group work, peer critique, and multiple drafts, creates a relationship between the known and the new that calls for pedagogical participation. Berlin explains:

> There are a number of qualifications I want to make in offering these new course outlines. Most important, I do not wish to present them as anything more than possibilities. Their purpose is finally illustrative rather than prescriptive. I hope that teachers will find in them suggestions for developing course materials and activities appropriate to their own situations. . . . I do want to emphasize, however, that the center of each course is the response of students to the materials and methods considered. (115)

Although Berlin has bracketed the theories that led to the pedagogy, teachers are positioned here as starting from rather than ending with his particular pedagogy. Significantly, students' responses to materials and methods, rather than their ability to adapt to them, is also positioned at the center of the composition classroom. These changes revise many of the unquestioned assumptions upon which the differences among student discourses, teacher discourses, and the professional discourses of the field are usually constructed. The idea that students can analyze course readings and other texts to see how meaning is encoded therein, for example, and that they can use those readings to generate heuristics, bridges the gap between reading and writing that informed first phase process movement models. A major taboo—the idea that nothing about writing processes can be learned from products—is exposed as false not only for teachers and scholars, but also for students. Since the reading/writing relationship constitutes one of the major generative strategies of our professional discourse, bridging this gap at the levels of pedagogy and classroom practice is a vital step, if we are to open invitations for participation in and contribution to that discourse (and to the field more generally) to undergraduate students.

THE *OTHER* SOCIAL TURN: REDEFINING THE TERMS OF/FOR COMPOSITION STUDIES THROUGH SERVICE LEARNING

The American Association for Higher Education, in cooperation with the National Council of Teachers of English and Campus Compact, published *Writing the Community: Concepts and Models for Service-Learning in Composition* in 1997. Obviously, many of us had been experimenting with community-based literacy projects before 1997, but this volume is significant not only because of the collaborative efforts that led to its publication but also because of the images of students and teachers presented in its essays. Here I will look specifically at the introduction to the collection and at three additional essays: Nora Bacon's "Community Service Writing: Problems, Challenges, Questions," Bruce Herzberg's "Community Service and Critical Teaching," and Linda Flower's "Partners in Inquiry: A Logic For Community Outreach." These texts are important because they clearly illustrate the ways that students can be positioned as doing more than merely consuming composition studies even though they simultaneously limit our attempts to invite students to participate in the discipline itself. In their introduction to the collection, the editors Linda Adler-Kassner, Robert Crooks, and Ann Watters state "the most immediate effect of service-learning is to rearticulate the college or university as part of rather than opposed to the local community" (4). They credit the move "away from training students in literary studies and toward general academic discourse or writing in/across the disciplines with "greatly increase[ing] the value of [composition] courses" (12). Whereas revisions to process like Berlin's focus on changes in the methodologies they present as pedagogical guidelines, Adler-Kassner, Crooks, and Watters note that service learning is

> a shift of theoretical orientations away from disciplinary objects seen in
> isolation (the "verbal icon" and so forth) toward an attempt to discover
> inter-relationships among and between knowledge groups previously
> conceptualized as isolated from one another. (14)

In this scene, divisions between campus and community "abet and accelerate the uneven development that will increasingly reify those divisions" (3). Citing Eli Goldblatt, they propose that "'to teach literacy within the confines of the college [is] to accept an impoverished account of literacy that claims text alone can provide the reader enough reality to read the world' (1994: 77)" (8). In other words, the divisions between campus and community construct literacy in limited, and limiting ways, ultimately leading to a kind of isolation that allows individuals to "hold contradictory ideas or attitudes, provided the ideas never come to consciousness simultaneously" (9). This ideological problem of isolation, and the knowledge produced within it, "tends to restrict the range of student contact to the campus," in ways that "define lasting limitations on an individual's sense of community" (3). Seeing and writing across these boundaries, then, necessarily puts those inside the academy in relationships with those outside the academy.

As Nora Bacon notes at the start of her essay, the construction of these relationships "fundamentally challenges some long-standing assumptions about writing and learning to write" (39). One of the major assumptions challenged by service-learning based approaches to composition studies is that programs using such approaches are "not only developed in response to composition theory" (39). They also grow "in response to observed needs" (39). The program Bacon describes grew in response to the fact that

> community organizations needed help with writing tasks, the staff of Stanford's Haas Center for Public Service saw that students needed opportunities for service experiences linked to their academic courses, and instructors in the English Department believed they needed meaningful writing tasks with audiences beyond the classroom. (39)

Bacon notes: "as the program expanded and we began to shape courses to accommodate community-based writing," faculty participants "learned how it blended—or collided—with the theories of writing that informed our teaching practices" (39). But teachers are not the only ones who are invited to think about the theories informing composition classrooms when community-based writing becomes part of the scene. I will quote from Bacon at length to illustrate this point:

Experience with community-based writing, then, gives us a new perspective from which to view academic writing. It denaturalizes academic writing, for us and for our students, introducing self-consciousness about the business of writing for a teacher. While the teacher is in some respects a unique sort of audience, whose interests and power impose a unique set of constraints, she is quite real, and the classroom is a real rhetorical context. Given the opportunity to reflect on academic writing in the light of an alternative rhetorical situation, students may interrogate the classroom as a context for writers: Why is writing valued in undergraduate classes? In what ways and to what extent do teacher expectations determine the context and form of school writing? Why is the essay the preferred genre in so many disciplines? What values are implied by the privileging of essays? What, in other words, is the relationship between the form and function of writing in other classes, or in particular nonacademic settings? (43)

Here, students and teachers are engaged, at least in part, in the exploration of a shared set of questions and issues relevant to composition studies itself: audience, the role of writing and writers in undergraduate education. One can imagine that both teachers and students might gain experiences here that could generate insights of importance to the discipline. In the end, however, Bacon decreases these possibilities by making two discursive moves. First, at the moment that she positions students as learners who might have something to contribute to the discipline, she argues that teachers need to "become students . . . not only of writing in the disciplines but of the communicative events, genres, and technologies that constitute writing outside the academy" (52). This would not be a problem except that it is paired with a simultaneous reconstitution of the traditional hierarchy of the student/ teacher binary by designating where the knowledge constructed by both parties will rest: "As they investigate questions such as these, students may develop an understanding of rhetorical variation that prepares them to navigate in multiple discourse communities. As we [teachers] participate in the investigation, we may extend and refine the theories of writing that inform our work" (53). As I illustrated above, at this point, teachers have already been put in the student role when it comes to developing the kinds of knowledge generated by the questions referred to here; this knowledge is at least shared by both parties. But extending and refining theory and the knowledge behind the scene of writing is more clearly reserved here only for teachers. In fact, the inscription of the theory-as-the-basis-for-new-knowledge narrative interrupts the possibility that students might contribute to the discipline in substantive ways by repositioning them as embodying and illustrating the effectiveness of theories and pedagogies that lead to their "increased navigational skills". Bruce Herzberg's essay focuses on a pedagogy that centers the study of "literacy and schooling" (59). In his description of the course, which requires students to do literacy tutoring in the second semester, he emphasizes that

> We do not set out to study teaching methods or composition pedagogy. The students learn some of the teaching methods they will need in tutor-training sessions that take place largely outside of class time. But in the class itself, our goal is to examine the ways that literacy is gained or not gained in the United States, and only in that context do we examine teaching theories and practices. (59–60)

The pedagogical aim here is an "attempt to make schools function . . . as radically democratic institutions, with the goal not only of making individual students more successful but also of making better citizens, citizens in the sense of those who take responsibility for communal welfare" (66). Raising "critical or cultural consciousness" is necessary to the endeavor because without this level of awareness, student responses will be "personal" in ways that block access to the underlying structures of social problems. With this awareness, students come to see problems as social rather than individual. "The final research papers for the composition course," then, "show a growing sophistication about the social forces at work in the creation of illiteracy" (66). They illustrate "a sense of life as a communal project, an understanding of the way that social institutions affect our lives and a sense that our responsibility for social justice includes but also carries beyond personal acts of charity" (66–67). Calling up Kurt Spellmeyer's use of the concept of the "social imagination," Herzberg ends not with a call for theory, but with an assertion about the importance of constructing relationships between known and new knowledge that challenge the naturalness of the way things are and open spaces for transformation.

> As Kurt Spellmeyer (1991) says, "the university fails to promote a social imagination, an awareness of the human 'world' as a common historical project, and not simply as a state of nature to which we must adjust ourselves" (73). Students who lack this social imagination . . . attribute all attitudes, behavior, and material conditions to an individual rather than social source. Students will not critically question a world that seems natural, inevitable, given; instead they will strategize about their position within it. Developing a social imagination makes it possible not only to question and analyze the world but also to imagine transforming it. (73)

What happens to the student papers that articulate this imagination in relation to the issues of school and literacy is not clear. Surely, the subject matter is important to composition studies, but there is no summary or evaluation of that content here. There is no indication that the knowledge generated therein has affected even the program from which the papers emerge, despite a hope for the effects their production might lead to in the larger culture. The papers possess radical potential, perhaps, but raising the consciousness of the writer seems to be their primary function. This is not an insignificant accomplishment, and Herzberg's work is impressive in its understanding of the ways that a variety of kinds of responses to the issues addressed in his class—personal, academic, activist—can lead to integrated knowledge for students. But in the end, in this narrative of the course, student discourses seem to have no place to go. The leap across the profession to "the world" is, in part at least, responsible for this dilemma. The places in which student discussions of the processes and content of the papers might have something to contribute—at conferences and/ or in professional publications of the field, for example—are filled with other concerns and by other voices. This is a serious issue to be sure, and not an easy one to address. What is important to note here is that the pedagogy sets up a situation in which composition studies does not model the very kinds of activities the pedagogy is aimed at, even though the processes and knowledge bases engaged for these purposes—and the products they produce—are relevant to the field. The work may help students see transforming the world as a possibility, but using it to transform composition studies is not their concern. In an odd way, their position in relation to the field mirrors the position the pedagogy is supposed to challenge in their relationships with the world.

Arguing for a "logic of inquiry," Linda Flower outlines an approach to service-learning in composition which "points to collaborative social action" (101). Before she outlines what she calls "the logic of prophetic pragmatism and problem solving," however, she finds it necessary to set aside the question of attempting to apply her work directly to the profession. This is not a criticism of Flower, who is well known for her collaborations and contributions to the field. It is, instead, a broader look at the source of the challenges we face in the process of inspiring our profession to live up to the potential we claim it can create in individual lives and/or in the world. The deferral of this potential as inscribed here is worth considering at length. Consider Flower's final statement about the "logic of compassion," one of the forms of logic for community service that she considers before she poses her own "logic of prophetic pragmatism and problem solving" (100).

> The logic of compassion and identity that is grounded in an alternative consciousness—at the same time it is shaped by religious tradition—works to reorient relationships away from cultural imposition, commodified service delivery, or expert, technology-driven knowledge transmission to ones that replace power relations with greater mutuality.
>
> But its strength also poses a problem. How do we translate this intensely individual consciousness into publication—into literate practices, educational agendas, and institutional initiatives? I ask this question not because there are no ready answers but because there are so many—competing—answers. Can we claim that any given literate practice or educational agenda has a corner on compassionate or democratic collaboration as we plan and argue for a course of action? Let me put our dilemma as educators and program developers another way. Given that our moral and ethical commitments are inevitably culturally inflicted, given that our best interpretation of what it means to

enact service, compassion or mutuality is itself a hypothesis to be tested and inevitably revised, how do we find the grounds for action? (100)

Once these professional and institutional matters are deferred, a variety of kinds of community problems can be addressed successfully. "[S]tudents, faculty, community leaders, and everyday people, as well as the written knowledge of the academy and the oral wisdom of the neighborhood" can come to the table "around the kind of issue that is both (1) an open question with no single answer and (2) a problem with immediate and local impact" (105). Of course, Flower is most likely assuming that changing the actual conditions within which the members of the writing classes exist is one of the consequences of engaging her approach. And, of course, introducing new voices into the discussion of problems in direct ways as well as through secondary texts creates new discursive possibilities. But the relationship between students in the composition classroom is still radically different in relation to the discipline than in relation to the community: the kind of mutuality held up as the goal outside of the student/discipline relationship is not held up as a goal within that relationship. Flower states: "A community problem-solving dialogue tries to bring the voices of academic discourse, as well as those of the people described by that discourse, to the table" (105). But I would argue that there is a very real sense in which the composition classroom would create just this mutual situation if much of the scholarship of the field were present in that space. The people described by our discourses (composition teachers and students) would hear the voices of those who do the describing. The problem, say, of the differences between and among the expectations of college writers as they are defined in a variety of these discourses and the impact of these descriptions on the lives of the students and teachers in the immediate institutional context might constitute the grounds for a "problem-solving dialogue." This creates the kind of community within the profession that service-learning attempts to create between university and neighborhood communities. These conversations might then be relevant to the profession and its constituents in the same ways that the products Flower describes are relevant to the lives of the members of the problem-solving dialogue groups she discusses.

EXTENDING PROCESS: A CASE STUDY OF BRUCE McCOMISKEY'S *Teaching Writing As A Social Process*

While "some post-process theorists seem to have followed Trimbur's lead in positioning the social outside of the process "paradigm," others, like Bruce McComiskey, have sought to define post-process not as the rejection of the process movement but as its extension" (Matsuda 73). This "extension" is illustrated in *Teaching Writing as a Social Process*, where McComiskey describes the theories behind his practices—both those he identifies with and those he does not—to create a pedagogical approach based on "aspects of social theories that . . . have important relevance for composition studies" (4). That McComiskey identifies with some aspects of process theory and not others, with some aspects of the social turn and not others, illustrates the complicated ways that those of us who were students in process classrooms as undergraduates and who continued our education in graduate programs in the field stand in relation to composition studies. Although he does not directly explore this fairly new situation in which the same people may have been students in process classrooms before they became members of the profession, his book demonstrates the ways that the hold "identification with" had on our subjectivities as undergraduate students was—or at least is—interrupted by our study of writing. McComiskey is overtly committed to empowering students in the ways he has been empowered by the process movement—albeit through different practices from those he learned as an undergraduate or graduate student. As McComiskey states, "most chapters [of the book] . . . present and illustrate heuristics for rhetorical inquiry based largely on . . . social theories" (4). Before he gets to this point and can move forward, however, McComiskey claims to be setting aside what he calls the "read-this-essay-and-do-what-the-author-did method of writing instruction" (1) that informs "social content" (2) courses. This rendition of what composition studies is about shares much with first-phase movement declarations: heuristics and process are prominent and the textual model approach is set aside. McComiskey's problem with the textual model approach is that such courses "miss the fact that critical theorists, like Barthes, Fiske and many others, develop over the years complex heuristics through which they approach their subjects" (2). Using Barthes as his example, McComiskey identifies the real problem: the products of these heuristics "actually mask the heuristic process that Barthes undertook to compose the published version of [*Mythologies*]" (2). McComiskey is correct, I think, to assert the difficulty of understanding heuristic processes in the texts he points to through isolated processes of reading the individual texts he holds up here. And although he will continue to use Barthes as his example, McComiskey implies that any classroom approach to composition that attempts to bridge the gap between reading and writing by examining texts to learn about heuristic processes "leaves students in 'social content' composition classes with an impossible task—write an essay like Barthes, but do it without the kind of heuristic processes from which he had to draw" (2). The idea that the writing class should become a place where these heuristics are studied, however, is not the pedagogical move McComiskey favors. There are a lot of assumptions operating here: assumptions about the kind of reading happening in "social content courses," assumptions about the knowledge of the teacher and his or her ability or inability to share that knowledge with students, assumptions about what counts as "social content." And these assumptions defer the possibility that the composition classroom should become a place where students study and develop complex heuristic processes rather than consuming and applying heuristic processes they had no part in developing. For the purpose of opening spaces for participation and contribution, however, we must focus our attention on the assumptions here about student abilities and about the appropriate way to position students in relation to the disciplinary knowledge behind the pedagogies they encounter. McComiskey is quite clear about this point.

> Assigned readings are neither the only nor the best social-process heuristics available to writers and teachers; social theory offers a wealth of critical methodologies for interrogating social institutions and cultural

artifacts, and these methodologies easily convert into rhetorical heuristics that guide writing processes in a variety of economic, cultural, political, and social contexts. (3)

This easy "conversion" takes place outside of the classroom, as its pre-text, if you will, reinforcing first-phase process movements' model for constructing pedagogy: the process applied in the classroom—even though accommodating of heuristic choices—is developed through work that goes on behind the scenes (and as an inscription of the teacher's authority). One might assume at first glance that this is a major stumbling block in creating spaces for participation and contribution. But this is only true if, once again, we defer the questions of participation and contribution in relation to composition studies. That is, throughout the rest of the book, McComiskey presents a pedagogy that leads to assignments inviting students to respond to the problems they identify in productive ways—mostly through letter writing. In these letters, students address audiences they believe can do something about the problems they have identified. They write letters to magazine editors, administrators, important people in companies of mass production, etc. They even write letters to teachers, educational administrators, etc., identifying specific campus problems and posing solutions. Behind these letters is a critical process that often includes readings of critical texts (especially in the sections about education) that situate the student discourses, but that are not present in or available through that discourse (see especially chapter 6 for examples). The letters are instances of the "mythologized" process McComiskey identifies as marking theory in the beginning of his book. It is not only the process that is hidden. What happens to the critical analyses behind these letters is unclear; perhaps they are circulated among class members and we can assume that they are evaluated and constitute part of the students' grades for the course. I do not mean to devalue McComiskey's work or the work of his students. In fact, and to the contrary, I want instead to value all of it as demonstrating the very real possibility that the work illustrates how much we have to gain from thinking of our undergraduate students, and especially our first-year composition students, as people who also have significant contributions to make to composition studies.

CONCLUSION

The chart below illustrates the ways that these pedagogies simultaneously value opening spaces for participation and contribution as vital components of composition studies, while remaining ambivalent about how those values relate to composition studies in ways that call us to rethink the student/discipline relationships within the field.

Things That Encourage Participation and Contribution as Valuable to Literate Activity	Things That Discourage Participation and Contribution in Relation to Composition Studies
Berlin	*Berlin*
The move from mastery to analysis	
The break between identification of and identification with	
Shared strategies for analysis and generation of texts	It is unclear where the resulting discourse goes
Closing the gap between analytic and generative tools available to theorists who inform pedagogy and those available to students	Preconstructing strategies from theories and texts students and teachers never look at together
Bacon	*Bacon*
Approaches to composition that are not based solely on theory and the needs of academics	Constructing navigation of multiple discourse communities as the end of composition studies for students
Shared comparative knowledge-building across different rhetorical situations within and outside of academia	Constructing extension and refinement of theories of writing informing composition studies as the work of people other than students
Herzberg	*Herzberg*
A study of literacy and schooling that raises critical or cultural consciousness	Brackets composition studies as affected by the study
Questioning and analyzing is not the end of the course; being able to imagine ways to transform the world is the purpose	It's not clear where this discourse goes

Flower	Flower
Brings academic discourse and those described in it to the table	Brackets the student/discipline relationship in favor of other relationships
McComiskey	**McComiskey**
Certain forms of student discourse go beyond analysis and beyond the classroom	Favors distribution of rhetorics that reinscribe traditional writer/audience relationships outside of the classroom
	Reading the texts behind the pedagogy not necessary for students (sometimes not necessary for teachers either)
	Conversion of texts informing the pedagogy does not occur in the classroom scene
Shared Traits	
1. The leap across the profession to the world 2. Relationship between student discourse and composition studies is left unexplored 3. Unclear student/discipline relationships in general	

Taken together, these revisions to process suggest that certain pedagogical approaches can open spaces for participation and contribution. They also illustrate that most who have attempted serious revisions to process theories, pedagogies and practices have understood participation and contribution not primarily in relation to composition studies itself, but in relation to other social spaces. This social turn is, then, in some ways, a turn away from attempts to center student writing in composition studies and a turn toward distributing it in other spaces. This shift represents a different turn toward product than the one identified by first phase process movement pedagogies and critiques of that movement, one that balances the writing/world relationship in new ways. In this turn toward product, pedagogies and student writing are evaluated according to their abilities to have effects outside of the disciplinary spaces of composition studies, its theories, pedagogies, and practices.

This turn away from a process/product binary makes sense within the history of a process movement that faced the challenge of rescuing composition classrooms from explication (e.g., for the purpose of self-exploration and revelation, meeting audience expectations, attending to writing across the disciplines, etc.). The urge to create relationships between student writing and the world beyond traditional classroom spaces and purposes is one important thread across attempts to challenge the images of students and teachers that arise within critiques of what became the dominant approaches to composition in the wake of first-phase process models. The practical strategies worth exploring here are the move from mastery to analysis; the creation of shared focuses for inquiry (between and among students, teachers, community members), cross-class work, exposure to some kind of community literacy activity; complex relationships to pedagogies; and the repositioning of critique as something other than the end of writing. We have so much to learn about centering student writing in new ways from engaging these revised approaches and the new possibilities they present us with. This is the transitional moment I am after, both in the sense that I come after others who started the trail and in the sense that it goes beyond me—and because it is what I will continue to work for. The next two chapters discuss a particular approach to the reading/writing dialectic that engages these possibilities for the specific purpose of opening spaces for participation and contribution to become defining features of the field for all members of the writing classes.

3

REVISING INVENTION, ARRANGEMENT, AND REVISION

As the previous chapter indicates, revisions to process model approaches to composition studies begin to open spaces for participation and contribution to become valued in composition studies. In this chapter, I will use one particular course as an example of how the concepts of invention, arrangement, and revision can help us center participation and contribution in composition classes. To make participation and contribution available subject positions for writing-class students, I assume that the move from mastery to analysis, the break between identification of and identification with, shared strategies for the analysis and generation of texts and positioning something other than analysis or critique as the end of composition studies are necessary activities. These revisions occur within a context that has favored limited subject positions for many members of writing classes. As Miller's work has shown, these limitations are in large part responsible for the creation of a genre of writing (i.e., student writing) that has no structural relevance for the writers outside of its function as a product for classroom evaluation. In her introduction to *Feminism and Composition Studies*, Susan Jarrett reminds us that

> in the 1970s, composition . . . discovered its subject in the students of the writing class and began asking them to tell their stories . . . and teachers began to shift the focus of reading away from literary texts and toward student texts, thus altering dramatically the canon of the writing class (5)

At the same time, however, composition studies continued to position students as "almost always outside the process of theorizing. [Therefore], the discourses of pedagogy speak themselves almost entirely in the absence of students . . ." (8). This theoretical subjugation rests in large part upon the specific ways that students are positioned (or not) in relation to the field itself through the pedagogies that inform their lives. Furthermore, as Stephen Parks reminds us, and as I have discussed at length in my introduction, these constructions of student writing subjectivity were also part of the larger conservatism of our professional organizations, especially the Modern Language Association, National Council of Teachers of English, and the Conference on College Composition and Communication (125–153). In addition, Mariolina Salvatori identifies the following structural features of first-phase process movement pedagogies as key "streamlining interventions" that restricted the subject positions available to first-year writing students: "the separation of reading from writing, the proliferation of specialized programs within departments, the reduction of pedagogy from a philosophical science to a repertoire of 'tips for teaching'" (WTS 174). As the revisions to first-phase process movement models show, these theoretical, political, and structural "streamlining interventions" become obstacles when we attempt to create more inclusive and empowering subject position for students in the field of composition studies.

The ways that the prewrite/write/rewrite model of composition studies creates and maintains these "streamlining interventions" and the restrictive subject positions of "student" in the systems they create must be challenged if we hope to make spaces for the voices of those traditionally excluded in the constructive activities that constitute the field. For within those restrictive approaches, students and teachers can consume and enact a model without any awareness of the disciplinary knowledge that led to its construction: neither teachers nor students read texts from the discipline, except, perhaps, texts that reduced writing pedagogy to "tips for teaching"; they didn't have to know anything about the field except, perhaps, the assumptions behind the particular first-year writing program within which they taught. These conditions were understood as necessary for two reasons. First, because reading was devalued as a way to learn about writing and, second because it was assumed that the teachers of first-year writing classes often had little to no background in composition studies, no interest in developing a meaningful relationship to the discipline, and no glimpse of the discipline beyond that presented in the textbooks they used. Positioning the field of composition studies as relevant to first-year writing classes would have been a ridiculous endeavor within this frame. Students and teachers are always already defined in relation to what they are assumed to lack: consciousness about and/or interest in composition studies, exposure to the discourses of the field, knowledge about the field more generally, and, ultimately the ability to participate in and contribute to the field in ways that challenge the positions that define and are defined by those lacks. Continuing to configure first-year writing courses as isolated spaces within which the need for the field simultaneously emerges and is repressed through the prewrite/write/rewrite model of process is questionable at best. Changing texts, or assignments, or writing practices in ways that do not alter basic assumptions about the literacy histories informing the lives of the people who constitute the field blocks approaches to composition studies that open spaces for participation and contribution. Stephen North has discussed this matter in relation to graduate studies in English, outlining the importance of graduate students in the construction of curriculum and the need for graduate studies to bridge the gaps between and among the territories of English Studies, and illustrating the ways discursive practices in graduate programs must change. But first-year writing students often face even more detached relationships with the discipline than do graduate students. This is the work that we have deferred, that we must now take up if we are to create a material reality within which our profession enacts many of the liberating and inclusive promises embedded in its history.

Creating introductions to writing that are based upon more realistic assumptions about first-year writing students' and teachers' positions as literate people who can participate in and contribute to, rather than merely consume or enact, composition studies is, I believe, vital to the profession and to the individuals whose lives are touched by the profession. For me, moving away from the prewrite/write/rewrite model as a teacher, scholar, and program administrator has been a vital part of beginning to open these spaces. I want to be clear that it was never my goal to move away from a commitment to exploring, researching, theorizing, and teaching writing as a process. Instead, my desire was, and is, to make composition studies more relevant to classroom pedagogies and practices, and classroom pedagogies and practices more relevant to composition studies. As Salvatori reminds us, this is not

> merely the question of whether reading should or should not be used in the composition classroom. The issue is *what kind of reading* gets to be theorized and practiced. . . . (1) Which theories of reading are better suited to teaching reading and writing as interconnected activities? (2) What is the theoretical justification for privileging that interconnectedness? (3) How can one teach that interconnectedness? (165–66)

For me, creating an approach that bridges the gap between reading and writing without setting aside the idea of process is vital as we respond to questions about the places and functions of reading in first-year writing classrooms.

If our selection of texts and our theoretical justifications for those choices fail to center composition studies in the composition classroom in ways that allow members of those writing classes to see the interconnectedness of their work and the field, for example, how can we expect the interconnectedness of reading and writing to be explored in and learned through the study of composition? This is a serious issue. Like many compositionists, I spent a short time at the beginning of my career thinking that my professional responsibility required me to start from the assumption that most teachers in first-year writing programs did not know the theories, issues, and practices of composition studies. I thought my job was to create pedagogical guidelines/tools, curricula, and program goals that did not require them to explore any of the major concepts of the field. In an odd way, and without meaning to do so, I was closing down opportunities for collaborative explorations of the history of literacy, the history of writing studies, and composition studies in general to become a central activity in the teaching of first-year writing for faculty in the same ways textbook approaches that I have outlined in chapter two closed down these opportunities for students. In the remainder of this chapter, I will focus on how I have opened the possibility of positioning students as something other than consumers of models. Chapter four will address the issue of opening the same possibilities for faculty of first-year writing classes through collaborative curriculum design and faculty development activities.

FROM PREWRITE/WRITE/REWRITE TO INVENTION, ARRANGEMENT, AND REVISION

I would not have begun to understand and challenge the assumptions behind the ways I had been trained to think about my role as a compositionist within classroom structures had I not grappled with these issues as a teacher of writing who is committed to opening spaces for participation and contribution to her students. That commitment led me to create a frame within which participation and contribution could also drive curriculum and faculty development. The approach itself grew out of an experience I had when teaching a "Theories of Grammar and Composition" course to English secondary education majors. (I was back at my undergraduate institution teaching the same course that had led to my own introduction to the field and to that important invitation to attend my first CCCC.) In that class, students read Peter Elbow's *Writing With Power* and Jonathan Kozol's *Illiterate America* to begin our discussions about the connections between the teaching of writing and our assumptions about teaching and learning. It became clear through class discussions that many of the students sensed that there were major differences in the ideas behind these texts, but that they were unclear about exactly what those differences were and/or how they could be read backwards to the assumptions driving their ideas about literacy, students, and the creation of writing pedagogies. To facilitate our progress, I asked students to join me in analyzing the invention, arrangement, and revision activities and strategies informing the texts. This felt a bit like heresy at the time. After all, the idea that we could learn anything about writing, especially about writing processes, from an analysis of products was not exactly encouraged in my education. In addition, I had to move away from the prewrite/write/rewrite model to open the discussion of disciplinary issues more generally in the classroom. We could not get at these connections just learning about prewriting strategies that may or may not have informed the texts of our literacy lives—especially since prewriting strategies were often prescribed in ways that favored activities that could not be discerned from the reading of products. I presented the following six questions and clarifications of them for our consideration:

- What is invention? (What did the writer have to do to create the text?)
- What's being invented? (What ideas, beliefs, world-views, and actions does the text call up?)
- What is arrangement? (How are things being put in relationship with one another?)
- What's being arranged? (What's being put in relation to what?)
- What is revision? (What is/has to be done to accomplish those changes?)
- What's being revised? (What changes is the author trying to inspire?)

What became clear to us right away was that the connections between what the author did to create the text and the activities proposed as solutions for writers and larger literacy problems were not always identical, or even necessarily compatible. But the most interesting thing that happened was that the exercise made it (painfully) clear that the notions of prewriting, writing, and rewriting presented in the composition materials we read represented only very limited versions of invention, arrangement, and revision informing the field of composition studies. For example, while it was easy to see how experience, reflection, a variety of kinds of primary and secondary research, and connection-making across areas of research were big parts of Kozol's process, it was not clear that any of these activities informed Elbow's process. In fact, it would be impossible to talk about Elbow's process at all, except perhaps to guess which, if any, of the strategies he instructs others to use might be informing his own process or to assume that he had read the twelve books in the "select annotated bibliography on publishing," and those from which he occasionally quotes (375). This got me thinking more generally about how dominant versions of "writing as a process" limited invention, arrangement and revision in the ways Richard Young, Janice Lauer, Sharon Crowley and others discuss previous historical restrictions of the art of invention. That is, the ways that composition students were invited to participate in composition studies through construction of the prewrite/write/ rewrite pedagogies of the first-phase process movement may have represented a new version of restricting students' (and teachers') access to the possibilities of participation and contribution in the same ways that previously critiqued models restricted their access to these functions of literacy. One of the most significant outcomes of the limitations we noticed was that student writing was restricted primarily to the revision of student texts, while both Elbow and Kozol could claim to be attempting to revise things like writers' processes, our understanding of the causes of illiteracy in America, and so on. The students were, of course, shocked and angered by the idea that they had been so strongly educated to construct such a limited idea of themselves as writers, and many were deeply concerned about reproducing this "student writer" in the classrooms they would enter as teachers.

Throughout that semester, I grew increasingly aware of why reading, especially the kind of reading that focused on texts as things we could learn about writing processes from, became a dangerous activity in the first-phase scenario. Reading texts designed specifically for use in the composition classroom as texts that call up certain writers and certain kinds of writing had to be deferred for that writer and "student writing" to emerge. This deferral shuts down many of the opportunities for discussing the issues, concerns, methodologies, and ways of writing that constituted—and still constitute—composition studies. It, therefore, also defines teaching and learning more generally in very limited ways.

I am reminded of these students' reactions and initial insights every semester when I present the six questions listed above to first-year writing students, who are understandably confused by the idea that we will use the same questions to think about reading and writing as we progress through the semester. In fact, a group of students in one of the honors sections of the first semester course recently asked me if I had made up the terms invention, arrangement, and revision to drive them all crazy, or if they had any connection to the other things they knew about writing (we were discussing Resnick and Resnick's "The Nature of Literacy," and they had tried to respond to the six questions as part of their preparation for the second day of class). I asked them what they knew about prewriting and in unison they responded, "outlining and brainstorming." A couple of students added clustering and journaling to the list. I asked them about organization, and again, in unison, they gave me the outline for a five-paragraph theme. I asked them about revision, and they were stumped until I asked them about editing and rewriting to meet audience expectations. As I explained that the prewriting strategies they named were small pieces of invention, that the organizational plan they named was one small slice of the larger issue of arrangement, that the rewriting strategies they named were a small slice of the larger picture of revision, they became somewhat agitated. At this point we had already been discussing the invention activities and arrangement patterns informing the essay we had read for that class; they did not want to discuss revision. They weren't ready. They wanted to know why there were such big differences between the writing activities informing the essay we had read and those they had learned and assumed would serve them well throughout their college careers. They were honors students, after all, and their advanced placement course had claimed to be preparing them for college writing assignments.[20] As we discussed the different things that "being prepared" might mean, for example—being able to do the same thing over and expect a successful outcome versus being ready to learn new ways of doing things—they became very quiet. One of the women in the class noted that the kinds of literacy discussed in the article included both of these ideas—literacy as a process of learning limited skills and literacy as the ability to function across lots of different situations—and she asked if that was why I had assigned the article. Another student wanted to know why "no one told us about this before," (a common question when I use this approach in all kinds of first-year and upper-division writing courses). Another student asked if this was why the authors of the article were against the "back-to-basics" movement. Another student asked if the class would be expected to use some of the writing strategies informing the article when they wrote their own papers, and we were off. Reading was no longer just about knowing what the article said and being able to represent that accurately, and writing was no longer about the reproduction of familiar ways of making meaning. Far from making things easy, the whole conversation had made things difficult. The students had asked me to prove the validity of the method in relation to their past experiences, future needs, and upon disciplinary grounds (they wanted to know how this method related to anything else they knew about writing and reading). At one point, a student had responded to one of the questions about arrangement by outlining the content of each section of the article, and when I asked her to tell us how each section was put in relationship with each other, she had become angry. She knew what the sections said and accused me of saying that her accurate repetition of that material was unimportant. As I repeated what I had said and apologized for making her feel that her comment was unimportant, other students began to realize the amount of distance the method put between them and the way of responding to readings they were used to, good at, and rewarded for in the past, and they began to worry about grades. Grades are a serious matter for our honors students, most of whom would not be able to attend the university without the financial support of the honors scholarships they receive and can keep only if their G.P.A. does not fall below 3.4. All of these issues arise in some form or another[21] when invention, arrangement, and revision are the focus of the class.[22]

Equally important is the way that focusing on invention, arrangement, and revision invites students and faculty in first-year writing classes to read the discourses of composition studies. For example, the first formal writing assignment in my first-semester writing course is often a literacy autobiography. We read many literacy autobiographies and excerpts from literacy autobiographies as we think about the assignment. Examples of such readings include excerpts from Mike Rose's *Lives on the Boundary*, Linda Brodkey's "Writing on the Bias," Richard Rodriguez's "The Hunger of Memory", Jennifer Lawler's "The Screenwriter's Tale," and Suzanne Sowinska's "Yer Own Motha Wouldna Reckanized Ya: Surviving an Apprenticeship in the 'Knowledge Factory.'" Our analysis of the texts allows us to identify some of the features of literacy autobiography without positioning mastery of those texts as the goal of our readings. Instead, our readings can lead to some observations about the ways literacy autobiographies are structured, the possibilities and limitations of those structures and the versions of the world they produce, and the ways that the invention, arrangement, and revision strategies therein might facilitate and/or obstruct our own processes. In the construction of their own individual literacy autobiographies students can practice some of the ways of making meaning we saw at work in others' texts and/or engage other strategies and/or both. When we turn around to make student literacy autobiographies the text of the course later in the semester, then, we can use an analysis of invention, arrangement, and revision to generate a picture of the starting places, movements, and relevance of those narratives to composition teachers, students, theorists, indeed, to composition studies. We can also discuss the ways that certain invention strategies support some narratives better than others, what is invented through the narratives, and the ways that the work invents new meanings, ideas, visions, etc. We can also move to discussions about invention, arrangement, and revision that inform the discipline. Articles about invention as discovery, insight, creation, etc. can be introduced as these issues arise in the course of our discussions. Discussions about form, organization, and the form/content relationship also become relevant, as do discussions about audience and revision. The texts of the discipline enter into the discussion as parts of a conversation rather than as prescriptions for practice. Students can enter into those conversations as writers and learners who have ways to understand, respond to, and contribute to those conversations. As the field becomes relevant to the classroom, the discourses created by those who constitute the class become relevant to the field.

Because students are tutoring people in general education diploma (GED) classes, English as a Second Language (ESL) classes and adult basic education (ABE) classes run by a local community literacy agency (more about this in the next chapter), they also see how the literacy histories of others construct and are constructed upon notions of literacy, access to literacy education, and other issues that deeply affect the reading and writing activities available to a variety of people. As a result, these students can tell us much about the local literacy context of the city where the university is located, and this knowledge gives them a variety of ways to contribute to conversations about university/community relationships, the role of activist-based work in the academy, the implications of using university resources (including their own time) to support untraditional teaching and learning activities, etc. They can contribute much, and many of my students have, by presenting at conferences, at academic and non-academic writing workshops, contributing overtly to my own writing processes and products in significant ways, and participating in discussions about curricular reform of the first-year writing program at the university. That they have limited access to the professional conferences, print and electronic environments that constitute the profession is a problem that limits their ability to communicate with members of the profession, but this does not limit the relevance of what they have to say to the profession. Even though we explore and confront the ways that student discourse has been, and largely still is, configured by the profession as something to talk about rather than as something to listen to, and even though we can see how the construction of the student as a writer and reader whose texts and literate activities live outside of the discourses that define the material realities of their literacy educations, and even though it becomes clear that this positioning of student writers and student writing contradicts much of what we have been told writing will give people access to, we do not, in general, come to believe that our texts are irrelevant to the profession. Again, this is partly because we do not need to identify with these restricted notions of student literacy to be successful. If some of our potential audiences (e.g., composition scholars) create a professional scenario within which constructing theoretical, practical, and pedagogical models that valorize teaching students in ways that make them the audience of composition studies without making the profession an audience for the student work it calls into existence, we need not reproduce this scenario through our own work and lives. Indeed, part of what we learn about is who gets opportunities to participate and contribute, who does not, and why. Neither the field of composition studies nor education in general is bracketed from these conversations. In the remainder of this chapter, I will present some student responses to questions about invention, arrangement, and revision to illustrate more fully the ways that such analysis invites transitions that help make composition studies the subject of composition classes while maintaining the process movement's focus on student discourse and diminishing the great divide between student discourses and the field of composition studies.

FROM PREWRITING TO INVENTION

Obviously, what materials we choose to use in our writing classes affect how near to or far from composition studies we situate the members of those writing classes. And while my own definition of the field is broad and flexible, including the study of literacy more generally, I do believe that we must challenge the notion that all discourse has an equal place in the first-year writing classroom. This challenge must be based, in part, on the fact that many of the teachers of those courses themselves have little or no background in the field and, therefore, must be considered learners and readers within the contexts of composition studies. Selecting materials that make the field available to the faculty, students, curricula, and other structures of higher education will, I believe, open spaces for participation and contribution to become central to our work. As Janice Lauer notes in "Rhetorical Invention: The Diaspora," "one of the long-standing conversations in composition studies has been the relationship between the creative and interpretive acts, between heuristics and hermeneutics" (10). Within contemporary critiques of composition studies, this conversation has taken decidedly divisive turns, often pitting rhetoric against composition and theory against discourses about teaching. In "Rhetoric and Composition as a Coherent Intellectual Discipline: A Meditation," C. Jan Swearingen proposes that within these recent divisions "as institutions, and institutional practices, rhetoric and composition seem poised for segregation, or divorce" (21). But this "segregation" is possible only when invention is conflated within pedagogical approaches that replace it with prewriting. Many students come to us with this limited notion of invention, one that positions them primarily as student writers who are consuming and adapting to a concept of "writer" that, like prewriting, offers only a limited view of the possibilities for invention, partly by positioning reading as a process through which we cannot expand our ideas of what it means to be a writer. These restrictions become apparent when we raise the issue of invention in classroom contexts. Here, for example, are the responses to questions about invention in Resnick and Resnick's "The Nature of Literacy" that one group of students constructed together on the second day of class:

What Is Invention?
Read and review previous scholarship on the issue from relevant sources.
Develop a knowledge of things (e.g. French history, etc.) in the article.
Put literacy artifacts and history and politics in relation to each other in each time period (also arrangement).
Develop a working knowledge of contemporary practices (e.g., "back to basics" movement).
Define what literacy means/is in each historical context.

What is being invented?
A picture of the differences among literacy practices and definitions across cultures and time periods.
The necessity to update the ways in which literacy is taught moving from elite to general public.
An educated argument using facts to persuade the audience.
An argument to both keep high literacy standards and educate all citizens.
The idea that even though U.S. has come a long way, many are still not literate.
A picture/scene in which "back to basics" movement is not appropriate for current U.S. context.

These responses allow us to begin a discussion of literacy and writing that makes what might otherwise seem like distant material close to our own experiences as writers and readers. As one student noted, the article talks about how certain kinds of literacy are kept away from "people like us" (i.e., those not from the upper classes) and the analysis of invention shows in more concrete ways what exactly is being kept away from us—certain ways of creating understanding, ways of making arguments about our own literacy experiences and what they do and do not allow us to "get practice doing." Another student made the comment that this seemed somehow like a bad thing to be doing—like "sneaking into writing." These are not unusual comments for the second day of class when I use this approach. Students begin to feel both afraid of what this might mean in relation to the ways of reading and writing they have become comfortable with and intrigued by the possibility that they may have cracked open some big literacy mystery. The fact that they have done the analysis themselves often becomes an issue. What if they aren't "right"? What if there are negative consequences to having the insights that result from the analysis? For example, what if they try these methods as writers and teachers punish them for trying to write like "real writers"? These are issues we will deal with all semester, inventing ways to understand different writing contexts and situations, others' expectations of us in those situations, and a wide variety of literate ways to construct our responses to those expectations (e.g., acceptance, rejection, redefinition, etc.). As Jarrett notes, "in the move from classical invention to composition's brainstorming, freewriting, and so on, there is a persistence of the assumption that knowledge is in the mind of the writer—we just have more 'inventive' ways of getting it out" ("Disposition" 70). But as we know, and as our work with students illustrates, confining writers to the knowledge in their minds—even though that may be what students expect of writing classes—restricts their ability to learn about writing (and about the knowledge in their minds more generally) from the texts they read, and it maintains a form of student writing that cannot hope to participate in and contribute to composition studies in meaningful ways.

FROM ORGANIZATION TO ARRANGEMENT

If we restrict our understanding of arrangement to the order of things within the text and/or to perfecting the forms of student writing, we restrict knowledge about arrangement in the same ways that process-model configurations of prewriting restrict invention.[23] In "New Dispositions for Historical Studies in Rhetoric," Jarrett "proposes using the term [disposition] in an analogical and imaginative way to inquire into the arrangement not only of ideas and language in texts but also of people and images in public spaces" (70) to "extend the inquiry beyond the immediate rhetorical situation to social relations more generally" (71). If, however, we focus on literacy in the composition classroom and ask questions about arrangement, we make the relationship between and among literacy, lived lives, and the structures that inform those lives the content of the composition classroom. If we double the question so that both what is being arranged and the methods of arrangement become clear, we can explore these relationships without losing a focus on writing. Such exploration is vital if we and our students are to understand the ways in which literacy refers to more than words on a page. Here are the students' responses to the arrangement questions about the Resnick and Resnick article (remember, this is only the second day of class and the first time students had practiced the method).

What is Arrangement?

Chronological historical periods

how the literacy program worked

how it was not successful for general population and won't work now

Put literacy standards in relation to personal accounts of individuals' literacy levels

Put each past practice in relationship to today's standards and needs.

What's being arranged?

Literacy criteria and social needs of the time are being put in relationship with one another.

Current literacy standards are being put in relationship with current practices.

Past influences of church, government, and military are being put in relationship with current influence of these organizations.

Class standing is being put in relationship with literacy levels.

Past literacy models are being compared to current literacy models.

Current elementary literacy level is being compared to level at the end
of the 19ᵗʰ century.

Teaching methods are being put in relationship with consequent literacy levels.

Quality of education is being put in relationship to capacity for individual growth.

Current ideas about literacy are being put in relationship with expectations for future needs.

Literacy levels are being put in relationship to standards/objective for
literacy.

As students noticed, the relationships under discussion in
the first part of our inquiry into arrangement do not always give
information or a picture of reality with which they can or wish to
identify. Their reactions revolved around one woman's comment
that the analysis had revealed "the big black dark secret of why
we think what we think." Students could relate the class-based
restrictions they were reading about to their own experiences as
student writers, even though they did not all necessarily identify as
members of the economic classes being discussed in the article as
having limited access to literacy education. This opened the door
for discussions about the ways literacy could be used both to create
and to close down opportunities for meaning-making (especially
making meaning about one's own experiences), could operate
both as an empowering and as an oppressive practice in any given
historical moment, and could invite reactions other than uni-
dimensional identification. In fact, the article itself is an exercise
in *identification of* that does not call for *identification with* everything
it presents, especially the historical practices and the ideologies
upon which they rest. Our discussions of revision more clearly
reveal how this break between *identification of* and *identification with*
becomes relevant to writing.

FROM REWRITING TO REVISION

Even during our first discussions of the Resnick and Resnick article,
students see that what the authors are supporting and what they
are challenging are in dialogue with one another. They can see that

the text invites us to revise our ideas about some of the main issues under discussion, and that revising those ideas implies other changes that must take place outside of the text. In addition, students begin to rethink their own literacy lives, often asking for time to discuss and identify the standards and expectations informing their own experiences. Such discussions often lead students to reflect directly upon the kind of analysis they are being asked to do for the class, especially as that activity relates to standards and expectations for their work. We can then begin to revise assumptions about what reading and writing instruction is/should/can be and to create a shared understanding of the goals for this stage of their literacy development. In fact, we can use the questions about arrangement to explore these issues and to discuss and practice the recursive and dialectical nature of the process of making meaning more generally. What kinds of things—criteria for evaluation, standardized tests, texts, etc.—did your literacy education put you in relationship with in the past and how were these relationships constructed (for example, through reading and writing assignments)? These conversations position students as people with information important to the course. They allow students and teachers to talk together about the study of reading and writing in ways that develop knowledge about the similarities and differences between and among their past ideas of themselves as literate human beings and other possible ways to think about the relationship between literacy and their own lives as individuals and members of larger social structures (educational, disciplinary, etc.). As student responses indicate, exploring issues of revision outside of their relationship to the rewriting of student texts opens many issues. Here are the student responses to questions about revision.

What is revision?

They wrote said article
Presentation of historical methods that aren't like ours
Used lots of different ways to present info (prose, charts, statistics)
Creating/presenting techniques in relation to how much they help us
    reach stated goals.

What is being revised?

Our idea of literacy–that lots of people are not literate when really our standards are just extremely high now

The idea that the back to basics movement is sufficient for educating towards literacy in our society today.

The idea that "functional" literacy can't get us where we want to be

The idea that any single historical definition of literacy is better or more appropriate for the current situation

As this one set of responses suggests, this approach to reading also calls for discussion of the connections between and among invention, arrangement, and revision. The focus on historical materials, for example, plays a role in invention, arrangement, and revision. The following chart makes these connections clear.

What is invention?	What is Arrangement?	What is revision?
Read and review previous scholarship on the issue from relevant sources.	Chronological historical periods	They wrote said article
Develop a knowledge of things (e.g. French history, etc.) in the article.	how the literacy program worked	Presentation of historical methods that aren't like ours
Put literacy artifacts and history and politics in relation to each other in each time period (also arrangement)	how it was not successful for general population and won't work now	Used lots of different ways to present info (prose, charts, statistics)
Develop a working knowledge of contemporary practices (i.e., "back to basics" movement)	Put literacy standards in relation to personal accounts of individuals' literacy levels.	Creating/presenting techniques in relation to how much they help us reach stated goals.
Define what literacy means /is in each historical context.	Put each past practices in relationship to today's standards and needs.	
	Current elementary literacy level is being compared to level at the end of the 19th century.	
	Teaching methods are being put in relationship with consequent literacy levels.	

What's being invented?	What's being arranged?	What's being revised?
	Quality of education is being put in relationship to capacity for individual growth.	
	Current ideas about literacy are being put in relationship with expectations for future needs.	
	Literacy levels are being put in relationship with literacy standards/objective for literacy.	
A picture of the differences among literacy practices and definitions across cultures and time periods.	Literacy criteria and social needs of the time are being put in relationship with one another.	Our idea of literacy—that lots of people are not literate when really our standards are just extremely high now
The necessity to update the ways in which literacy is taught moving from elite to general public.	Current literacy standards are being put in relationship with current practices	The idea that the back to basics movement is sufficient for educating towards literacy in our society today.
An educated argument using facts to persuade the audience.	Past influences of church, government, and military are being put in relationship with current influence of these organizations. Class standing is being put in relationship with literacy levels.	The idea that "functional" literacy can't get us where we want to be
An argument to both keep high literacy standards and educate all citizens.	Past literacy models are being compared to current literacy models.	The idea that any single historical definition of literacy is better or more appropriate for the current situation
The idea that even though U.S. has come a long way, many are still not literate.		
A picture/scene in which the back-to-basics movement is not appropriate in current U.S. context		

When students and teachers explore the connections between and among the implied activities behind texts, the relationships created by texts, and the revisionary purposes of texts, they begin to see process and product as connected endeavors. Rather than pretend that any process can lead to any kind of text, or that any one process can lead to any kind of product, or that any product is not the result of serious decisions one makes about process, students and teachers can make the exploration of such issues the content of their writing classes. In addition, many of the issues theorized as important to composition studies come to the foreground when texts are read as instances of process: purpose, purpose/reader relationships, methods of exploration, organization, history, known/new relationships, and different ways to present information to name a few. Obviously, different texts will foreground different concerns just as different assignments will offer (or disengage) opportunities to explore and practice different ways of writing. When we move from prewrite/write/rewrite models to invention, arrangement, and revision, we can select texts that raise the concerns of composition studies in composition classrooms according to the contextual needs of those classrooms without effacing the field. Again, this approach does not assume that the field is fenced in and that only certain parties and their discourses have the key to the gate. Instead, it begins from the assumption that all members of the class can participate in the field and have the potential to contribute in meaningful ways. This is, perhaps, the most important reason for moving away from the prewrite/write/rewrite model of process and toward approaches to composition studies that focus instead on invention, arrangement, and revision. Whereas the first set of terms present composition studies as settled by the time it gets to the level of classroom practice, the latter set centers composition studies as the area for exploration in the composition classroom. Within the larger context of our literacy histories, prewriting emerges as a very small representation of invention, writing emerges as a very limited notion of the issues surrounding matters of arrangement, and rewriting emerges as a constricted notion of revision.

This is not a traditional construction of disciplinarity or of the terrain of a field. In such scenarios, turf wars always already leave out the voices of many whose literacy lives are and will be affected by the environments created by the conflicts, partly as a way to claim rights to defining what the relevant conflicts will be. The contradictions and conflicts between our own writing practices and those we hold up as vital components of the teaching of composition are buried within our restricted constructions of students (and teachers) as writing subjects with little to contribute even though they constitute the majority if we count first-year writing as part of the field. Even a cursory look at the professional discourses of the field and at popular writing textbooks will illustrate this point. If we rethink the relationship between the discourses of composition classrooms and the discourses of the field, we will be able to include the discourses of the field in composition classrooms, and, consequently, to understand the relevance of classroom discourses to the field in new ways. (Re)positioning invention, arrangement, and revision of discourses about literacy as we continue to focus on writing as central to our endeavors is a transitional act; it begins to create the possibility of active agency for members of writing classes who have previously been constructed as concerned about—and in need of—a deferral of the discipline as readers and writers.

Because invention, arrangement, and revision were restricted in prewrite/write/rewrite models of composition that dominated the dissemination of writing as a process in first-phase movements, a more inclusive notion of these major terms, and of the discourses of the field more generally, must now come to inform our practices. By creating such transitions, we are positioning nearly all of the work of the field as important to our understanding of the assumptions, histories, habits, traditions, rebellions, conflicts and common grounds that inform the literacy lives of the people who constitute the field. Consequently, the work that occurs in the field can contribute in both broad and specific ways as we struggle to make spaces for new forms of participations and contribution. For example, within this frame the literacy histories of our students, the similarities and differences of those histories within and across our classes, the cultural, historic, economic, and political factors informing their constructions, the narrative patterns they create, and their place in the discipline are as important to our work as are the histories, ideologies, pedagogies of the field that we have tended to create outside of those histories. At the same time, and in a parallel way, the focus on literacy makes the history of writing broadly conceived relevant to the discourses of our students, and it invites them to help us all understand our literate lives within these disciplinary contexts. Imagine composition studies at the heart of the composition classroom; imagine the composition classroom at the heart of composition studies. The effects would be so dramatic that perhaps, in time, most teachers of first-year writing could base their courses on the knowledge of the field; and, perhaps their own knowledge of the field would at least match their knowledge of Madonna, or horror films, or TV shows or whatever other topic they choose to define as the content of their writing classes.[24] In addition, many of the issues we argue are important—personal narrative, the history of literacy, the previous education of our students and its relationship to our teaching and learning goals, writer/reader relationships, document design, style—emerge from our discussions if we make composition studies the focus of the course. These possibilities are enriched by the selection of texts from across genres. If we analyze one or two academic texts about literacy and then turn to some literacy autobiographies as students prepare to write their own literacy autobiographies, we begin discussions about the variety of approaches, texts, and literacy experiences that inform our literate lives. Looking back at the texts of our literacy educations—children's books,[25] student work from elementary and high school years, report cards, family scrapbooks—we begin to see the texture of our lives as literate individuals. Understanding these things in the context of our own pasts, one another's histories, the institutional criteria that define our abilities in school, and larger cultural contexts can become the focus of our explorations when the work of the field informs the composition classroom. Looking at the present and our futures as literate individuals as unlimited by those histories opens spaces for us to participate as we revise our ideas of ourselves as literate people. Far from decentering student writing, this work emphasizes the ways that different invention, arrangement, and revision strategies generate constructions of literacy in ways that invite us to do something other than identify with the status-quo literacy expectations for ourselves and one another. As I will illustrate in the next chapter, an approach that focuses on literacy and invention, arrangement, and revision also creates transitional spaces for teachers of composition who have literacy histories that are not informed by significant involvement in the discourses of the field.

TURNING TO WRITING

Because invention, arrangement, and revision can be used as generative as well as analytic heuristics, this kind of approach helps us move between reading and writing as people who have knowledge about the relevance of our experiences with literacy. In this way, no member of the class is positioned as an empty or flawed literate subject who must start at step one despite years of life as a literate individual.[26] This brings the relationship between known and new knowledge and expectations to the front of interactions between and among members of writing classes. Moreover, it does so in ways that deconstruct the assumption that identification can, does, or should define the major route to literacy. As the readings and exploration of the histories of literacy informing our lives will have illustrated, individuals and groups will have some experiences that call up some other form of subjectivity (e.g., resistance, false assumptions). In this way, we move away from analysis as the end of composition studies, especially for student writing, and toward generative analytics that take revision as their primary concern.

The first writing assignment, then, is a literacy history that invites exploration of the invention, arrangement, and revision activities that have informed students' attempts at personal narrative and a comparative analysis of the similarities and differences between those strategies and the strategies at work in the histories and literacy autobiographies we have read. Some students will decide that they must do memory work to begin the process of writing, others may have a clear idea of what they wish to revise, and others may decide that there is a specific relationship they wish to begin from. For example, students who have lots of artifacts from their literacy pasts (e.g., children's books, photographs, past successful and/or unsuccessful pieces of writing, etc.) often wish to begin by remembering the significance of those artifacts in their lives as readers and writers. Some students begin with the desire to revise their image of themselves as unsuccessful readers and writers or as individuals whose literacy skills are fine the way they are and should not require further attention. Still others will want to begin by exploring the relationship between the books they have identified with in the past and their literacy lives, or between their positive experiences in English classes and their assumptions about their potential as readers and writers. In each case, we can explore which kinds of invention strategies from our pasts, our current study of literacy, and from other sources in our literate lives might help each of us to invent in relation to our generative purpose(s). In addition, we have some ground for understanding our generative activities in relation to the larger discussions and assumptions about reading and writing that we have come in contact with. We can, therefore, begin to understand the relevance of our own discussions within those larger contexts; this is often a significant event for first-year writing students who tend to think that course readings can illuminate their own experiences, but that their own experiences cannot illuminate those discussions. Opening spaces that allow us all to see the larger relevance of what students have to tell us about their lives as literate individuals who come to our classrooms must precede theorists' and teachers' attempts to construct ourselves as audiences of student discourses. We cannot sidestep this issue by requiring students to take audiences other than their writing teachers as their pretend or real readers (especially real readers who do not evaluate the text for a grade if the text will be graded). Paradoxically, deferring teachers and the discipline as audiences for student writing operates partly to make student writing irrelevant to the field.

Of course, and as I have said earlier, this means that students and teachers face the realities of the profession—that it is not likely to become an audience for student discourse in the immediate future in the same ways it has agreed to become an audience for Rose or Rodriguez or Brodkey or Parks or Flower or hooks or

Woolf. But we do not have to interpret this fact as rendering the discourses of our classes irrelevant to the field. We can, instead, center that fact as a vital part of our understanding of literacy. That is, we need not simply identify with our position in this system; we can, instead, explore its implications and, if we desire, find ways to make our discourses participate in and contribute to composition studies in broader ways. This theme of the problems and promises of participatory literacy reverberates throughout our time together in a variety of ways, some of which help us to understand ourselves as able to use literacy to participate and contribute more than others. Community literacy tutoring, for example, allows us to participate in helping others meet their literacy goals as adult learners even as our own study of literacy finds its way into that work and as the students we tutor and their texts contribute to our understanding of literacy. Because this relationship is much more dialectical than is our relationship with the field, it gives us the opportunity to see that literacy can rest upon different kinds of relationships than those that position learners as consumers who do not need to participate and/or contribute to be part of the systems of learning informing their educations. Because we are tutoring, we face the realities that replicate those conditions for others and the challenges of not replicating these limited options for literacy with the learners we assist, and so we come to understand the nature of the struggle from multiple angles.

We turn to writing then, within the larger context of our lives as literate people whose individual and collective histories can be explored and understood in relationship to a variety of conditions. How we process that knowledge and the products of our processes can also be understood in a variety of ways and can begin to clarify the possibilities, obstacles, and opportunities encouraged and discouraged by those conditions. Furthermore, we begin to be more conscious about how our responses to these conditions can engage other routes to subjectivity—resistance, participation, and a desire for inclusion and contribution, for example—than those we are in the habit of assuming and/or believing appropriate. It is within this frame that we turn to writing, that new contexts for the activities of writing classes can emerge as transitional moments that do not require us to claim transformative power for ourselves and/or our pedagogies while leaving the structures that define a majority of our population in less empowered positions as members of the writing classes.

In the next chapter, I will describe a curriculum that both opens the possibilities for participation and contribution to become features of the first-semester writing classroom while attempting to maintain some recognizable relationship to the types of first-year writing pedagogies that are familiar to many people who teach and learn in those classes. I present detailed descriptions of individual writing assignments, activities, and faculty and community collaborations that create a context within which the shared and complementary knowledge of teachers and students centers participation and contribution in composition studies.

4

REVISING CURRICULUM

The challenges of directing first-year writing programs staffed primarily by people whose knowledge about composition studies is limited, and whose real interests lie elsewhere, are currently a reality in our field. But looking at the invention, arrangement, and revision activities apparent in the work that faculty do inside and outside of the composition classroom, and articulating the ways that the issues in that work relate to composition studies and the teaching of writing, allows us to bridge the gaps too often accepted as necessary for and by first-year writing teachers. The professional, individual, and programmatic problems of staffing first-year courses with adjuncts are well documented. However, if curriculum building, collaborative and cross-class work, and integrating varied interests in relation to the field become the grounds of composition studies, it will be less acceptable to construct first-year writing teachers as people who come in to teach individual classes and more important to think of them as people who come to participate in and contribute to a program. In this chapter, I focus on the ways that rethinking the first-semester course to open spaces for student participation and contribution can (and should) also invite faculty to participate in and contribute to composition studies. In my experience, guidelines and goals for first-year programs too often exist solely in relation to what types of texts students are supposed to be able to produce and not enough in relation to:

1) The goals for the faculty who teach the courses and the hopes for addressing the inequities embedded in the program (especially in programs staffed by adjunct and/or part-time faculty who desire full-time employment and all of the benefits it affords)

2) The creation of programs that integrate faculty interests in ways that inspire collaboration across sections of the course and

3) The relationship between the work that happens in first-year writing classrooms and the development of composition studies more generally.

If, as Sharon Crowley argues, the first-phase process movement was more successful at creating a profession than it was at changing the teaching of writing in significant ways, it created that profession in some fairly traditional ways ("Current-Traditional"). For example, it created institutional hierarchies, publication practices, and reward systems that did not challenge many of the assumptions about student discourse and its role in the profession, failing to open new subject positions not only for students but also for many teachers. In "Coming to Terms: Theory, Writing, Politics," Lynn Worsham compares this trajectory to the one taken by literary studies:

> For the last thirty years, composition studies has labored tirelessly to claim a place in the university as a legitimate academic discipline. We have been focused, in other words, on defining and legitimizing our work, on professionalizing ourselves in the context of the university culture and conventions. With single-minded purpose, we have sought to stand beside literary studies, as one scholarly profession among others, with our own ways of doing business with texts, and our own expertise. We have marked success in the usual ways: by the proliferation of graduate programs; the increase in the number of tenure-earning faculty positions held by composition "specialists"; the creation of a modest number of distinguished chairs for our own coterie of academic "stars"; and the increase in the number of scholarly journals and book series devoted to writing. (102)

In leaving these structural assumptions and positions unchallenged, the profession set a conservative trajectory for composition studies. But the process movement cannot be contained in this traditional way, partly because it invites us to acknowledge the multi-vocal nature of literacy, partly because it makes present the absent possibilities for expression and critical literacy suppressed by previous dominant models, and partly because it itself is a complex approach based not only on identification of and with prescribed standards, norms and practices. Most important, however, the process movement cannot be contained by traditional constructions of disciplinarity because the literate spaces opened by that movement invite individuals, groups, and the field to understand themselves as able to do something other than consume and adhere to prescribed norms and standards. Instead, it encourages integration of the areas of English Studies most often separated from one another to create institutionalized structures: reading and writing, the literary and the rhetorical, student discourses, teacher discourses, and the discourses of the field. The frustrations that we experience when these possibilities come up against a material reality that constructs the discipline as unable to accommodate these possibilities are very real. The responses I suggest acknowledge this frustration and work toward changing these material conditions. I am challenging some basic assumptions, but the commitment to changing the conditions of first year writing in ways that empower and are empowered by its constituents is not in conflict with the process movement. The idea that change can happen, that it can be positive and productive, and that it can help us make room for a variety of voices and more egalitarian literacy practices is integrated in and fundamental to composition studies. To enact this fundamental commitment, however, we must work toward transitions that alter the communal spaces that constitute the field. Here, I hope to show how five specific factors—reading, writing, community-literacy activities, cross-class activities, and collaboration—can foster views of literacy, environments, and revisions that open spaces for contribution and participation to faculty as they open these spaces for students. To make these transitions, we must create introductions to writing that are based upon these activities; only by doing so can we refigure our ideas about the potential for participation and contribution. Such refiguring is, I believe, vital to the life of the profession and to the individuals whose lives are touched by the profession. They are critical activities, not in the sense that they favor critique and its products, but insofar as they 1) position understanding of the field as important to the teaching of writing, and 2) create spaces for participation and contribution that do not pre-scribe identification with as the only or valorized route to subjectivity for members of the writing classes. In what follows here, I will use materials from interviews with two colleagues who have been collaborating with me to create and teach a first-semester course that engages the invention, arrangement, and revision strategies discussed in the previous chapter. As I have been illustrating, opening conversations about invention, arrangement, and revision gives us new ways to create relationships between and among the members of writing classes. There are other shared and complementary aspects to the course, as will become clear throughout my descriptions. While I will use specific examples from my own institutional context to illustrate my points, I am not proposing that every institutional context can or should open spaces for participation and contribution in composition in the same ways. In fact, in any particular context one will have to pay attention and take the risks involved in collaborative curriculum building to center composition studies in the composition classroom and meet these goals. Things that can't be orchestrated will come into play. Three activities, however, are critical to the collaborative endeavor:

1) Viewing writing within the larger literacy contexts informing people's lives
2) Creating an environment that allows teaching and learning to occur in ways that reflect the multiple and varied possibilities of literate action
3) Revising writing in light of 1 and 2.

These activities are critical because they are what people in composition studies do: we look at and try to understand literacy contexts in ways that help us foster and engage literate action, and we work together to revise composition in relation to what we see and the possibilities called up by what we see. If we look at literacy contexts in limited ways, for example, as determined by modes of discourse whose conventions are set and static, the possibilities for literate action will be defined by adherence and conformity, and the teaching of writing will be a process of reproducing those conventions. In fact, if we conflate composition studies to any one method of looking, practicing, and/or responding to invitations for literate action, we misrepresent the discipline and its endeavors. We may be "teaching writing" within whatever limitations we choose or are required to apply when we conflate things in these ways, but we are not doing composition studies. That this repression of the field leads to feelings of disconnection for members of writing classes—teachers and students alike—should be no surprise. In such scenarios we don't illustrate or practice what it means for our explorations of a subject to connect people to disciplines and their practices, nor do we invite people to explore the relationships between what is configured as disciplinary knowledge inside academia and their larger social contexts. Instead, we pretend that deep knowledge about the terms and possibilities for participation and contribution are not necessary or will happen somewhere else and that, therefore, it is not our responsibility to open these spaces for our students, our colleagues, and ourselves. I can't stress enough how important it is to consider composition studies as the opening of these spaces for participation and contribution, and to think about the success of the discipline in relation to these openings.

Let me emphasize that I am not arguing that any one- or two-semester course or sequence can invite an individual to become an active agent in composition studies as it is currently configured, especially if the discipline continues to become professionalized in traditional ways. What I am arguing is that participation and contribution are critical concepts in learning processes that do not restrict teacher/learner relationships to consumption and reproduction. The idea that we come together to participate in and contribute to knowledge bases, pedagogies, value systems, and structures of learning is vital in first-year writing courses, where students are introduced to the expectations of composing (in) higher education, and where many faculty are introduced to the expectations they can/should have for students and themselves as members of the composition community.[27] The approach to first-year writing presented here was designed to create collaborative spaces within which interested faculty could construct sections of a first-year writing sequence that would use shared and complementary materials and assignments to center participation and contribution as vital components of literacy. We did so despite the fact that each of us had experienced the field as uninterested in our discourses and the discourses of our students in many different ways.

I present these ideas not as guidelines to be followed, but as one way to think about the transition toward more inclusive composition practices. How one moves outside of the naturalized assumptions about writing classes matters less at this point in our history than that we make the move.[28] Opening spaces for participation and contribution means finding ways to let reading and writing exist in different relationships than those usually favored in writing classrooms. In addition, thinking about more than reading and writing, in this case cross-class work, collaboration, and community-based literacy activities, gives us more realistic ways to understand the literacy contributions and needs of members of our classroom communities and the larger communities to which they belong. Cross-class work, for example, pushes us to think about our students as a discourse community in new ways, ways that allow literate activities to cross the material boundaries that are composed when writing classes are configured as isolated spaces (sometimes even as we position reading about boundaries as a core course activity). The uneasiness we all feel when we try to talk across the boundaries that keep teachers and students in different sections of the course separate from one another (whether they are sections of students and teachers segregated by placement into different kinds of sections, e.g., honors, basic writing, standard sections, or sections within these segregated communities) opens all kinds of spaces for conversations about boundary crossing, the terms upon which boundaries are set up, and the ways we might interrupt the maintenance of those boundaries. Approaches that invite us to participate in such activities, forums in which our experiences as teachers and learners are informed by activities that speak to the real, present potential for boundary crossing called up by writing, enriches our study in many ways. The material, conceptual, institutional, social, psychological, and historical terms of the boundaries become clear as our reading, writing, and experience put us in contact with the ways that those boundaries are manifest in our lives and the lives of others as literate people in our communities.

Equally important is the fact that challenging the class boundaries of academia in these ways gives us a chance to practice crossing boundaries, to build knowledge together about the obstacles and benefits of such work, and to struggle toward common grounds for overcoming the limitations of a culture that has tended to use literacy education to segregate teachers and learners from one another (e.g., tracking, isolation of different kinds of learners from one another, administrative practices, etc.).

REVISIONING READING/WRITING RELATIONSHIPS

The assumption that we cannot learn anything about the act of writing from reading is part of the larger context within which the prewrite/write/rewrite model of process becomes dominant. This construction of literacy as necessarily informed by a split between reading and writing has done much to position faculty and students in non-participatory ways. As James A. Reither notes in "Writing and Knowing: Toward Redefining the Writing Process," this view of reading and the model of process it endorses,

> precisely because it has taught us so much—has bewitched and beguiled us into thinking of writing as a self-contained process that evolves essentially out of a relationship between writers and their emerging texts. That is, we conceptualize and teach writing on the "model of the individual writer shaping thought through language" (Bazerman, "Relationship" 657), as if the process began in the writer (perhaps with an experience of cognitive dissonance) and not in the writer's relationship to the world. In this truncated view, all writing—whether the writer is a seasoned veteran or a "placidly inexperienced nineteen-year-old" (Shor 72)—begins naturally and properly with probing the contents of the memory and the mind to discover information, ideas, and language that are the substance of writing. This model of what happens when people write does not include, at least not centrally, any substantive coming to know beyond that which occurs as writers probe their own present experience and knowledge.[29] (288)

The results of literate behavior in this scenario rest upon, and constitute, a disconnect between "the writer" and larger conversations and routes to participation. The faculty I have been collaborating with agree that the assumptions about the relationship between reading and writing buried within this model have caused major problems for them as teachers whose areas of interest seem to exist far outside of composition studies even though half of their load requires them to teach first-year writing. Configuring the course as a place where "literature" faculty step in and follow models for teaching writing that are not concerned with the integration of reading and writing has made the faculty I work with feel disempowered in the composition classroom, as if they have to choose between their areas of expertise (in these cases the study of eighteenth-century literacy trends and post-colonial literature, respectively) and teaching writing.

In my discussions with faculty, they often indicate that even though the teaching of writing is expected of them, the training, approaches, and methods of doing so that are common in their experiences have not encouraged them to see the teaching of first-year writing as part of the intellectual terrain of the field—even though their training has made them critical of the approaches and methods they have been mentored in and have seen others practicing. The split between reading and writing about the teaching of composition and doing the teaching is called up by models that rest on a more generalized split between reading and writing, which themselves rest upon the idea that the specialized areas of English studies that first-year writing teachers bring to the endeavor do not share any common ground upon which pedagogies of composition might be based. Challenging these splits began for us when I developed a way to set aside the dominant, pre-scribed notions of writing as a process without setting aside the notion of writing as a process. Equally important was a commitment to doing so in a way that would bridge the gaps between reading and writing that I had come to understand as severely limiting in my own life and in the lives of my students and colleagues. I was frustrated with the ways the splits between reading and writing misrepresent how the discipline of composition itself has been constructed through readings of classical texts, student texts, cross-disciplinary texts about writing, cognition, creativity, and theory (even though it tended to encourage only the reading of textbooks and student papers written for the course in first-year composition classes). This split creates and maintains gaps between faculty areas of interest and teaching responsibilities that are not addressed by models of process that assume no common ground between and among the diverse areas of interest held by people who teach first-year writing. As Mariolina Salvatori reminds us, this less than integrated configuration of literate subjectivity began to be challenged in the 1980s:

> Instead of being seen as an intrusion onto the field of composition, or a pretext for paying attention to something other than student's writing, as in the thinking of the 1970s, reading reseen in the 1980s through new theories and practices, was now appealed as a means of "bridging the gap" between the two activities and disciplines, a way of paying attention to reading and writing *differently?*[30] (165–66)

As Salvatori further notes, however,

> It is one thing to say that, even to articulate how, reading and writing are interconnected (as most of the authors featured in *Bridging the Gap* and *Reading and Writing Differently* do); and it is another to imagine and to develop teaching practices that both enact and benefit from the interconnectedness. (168)

Salvatori and others enact this interconnectedness by proposing staged assignments that ask students to read and reread texts, tracking the moves they make as readers.[31] But focusing only on student readings and/or proposing reading processes that do not also help faculty and students understand, practice, and participate in composition studies is shortsighted at best. At worst it extends to faculty the limiting notion of student subjectivity that Susan Jarrett, Susan Miller, Linda Flower, Bruce McComiskey and others interested in revising process identify in their work. When positioned as people who embody a method or model of writing, teachers, like students, enact rather than analyze the materials of the writing class. In other words, the discourses of composition pedagogy are also often spoken in the absence of the majority of people who teach first-year writing courses and, as Salvatori notes, if we want to invite faculty and students to participate in rather than merely enact writing pedagogies: "We cannot afford not to come to terms with the consequences of these streamlining

interventions (. . . the separation of reading from writing, the proliferation of specialized programs within departments, the reduction
of pedagogy from a philosophical science to a repertoire of "tips
for teaching") (174).[32] As Michael W. Kline notes in "Teaching a
Single Textbook 'Rhetoric': The Potential Heaviness of the Book,"
these "streamlining interventions" have often led to:

> rhetorics [that] avoid acknowledging their status as arguments, as
> deliberative claims that derive from value-laden warrants; instead,
> they posture as authoritative and mysterious texts, prescribing writing
> [and teaching] behaviors and establishing standards of good writing
> [and teaching] without revealing how and why the values underlying
> the advice they give were constructed historically in discourse about
> rhetoric. (139)

That early process-model interventions have led to these "mys-
terious" rhetorics is a serious matter not only for students, but also
for first-year composition faculty who tend to use such textbook
rhetorics to direct their own reading, writing, and pedagogies.
What we need, then, is an approach to first-year composition that
simultaneously opens spaces for participation and contribution
for teachers and students. This means that our ideas about curriculum and program development cannot ignore the fact that the
field is made up of teachers and students whose lives are seriously
affected by the material conditions of our first-year writing programs, including the reading materials we choose to include and
exclude in those courses. Considering the members of the writing
classes and the goals set for their interactions in relationship to
one another is one way to begin creating the kind of professional
sphere called up by composition studies.

What happens when we begin to set aside composition textbooks that suppress the history of composition studies and favor
models of first-year writing that position first-year writing students
and teachers as people who lack skills, exposure to composition
studies, and, ultimately, the ability to participate in and contribute to composition studies? What would happen if we acknowl-
edged the rich variety of literacy experiences and abilities that
students and teachers bring to first-year courses, and focused on

putting those rich histories in relation to composition studies in ways that invite participation and contribution? What would happen if we made the fact that formal education has seriously limited how those experiences and abilities can and do inform our knowledge bases, abilities, and opportunities for practice the major concern of first-year writing? To begin exploring these questions, we must stop configuring first-year writing courses as isolated spaces within which the subjects of composition are continually deferred—with disciplinary matters repressed within the prewrite/write/rewrite model of process and writing students restricted to producing texts and other literacy events that don't go anywhere. This is, in fact, the major reason we must move away from a prewrite/write/rewrite model of process: its repression of the field at the level of practice is the major source of limited notions of literacy in first-year writing courses. It institutes a theory/practice split that separated the field of composition studies from the teaching of first-year writing (more about this split in chapter five). Changing texts or assignments or writing practices without working to change the disciplinary context within which those things emerge and without altering basic assumptions has blocked revisions to composition studies that could define participation and contribution as goals for all members of the writing classes. As I noted in the previous chapter, Stephen North has discussed this matter in relation to graduate studies in English, commenting briefly on the ways members of the discipline must reconfigure English studies to include careers outside of academia (such as careers in community literacy agencies) and outlining in more detail the ways discursive practices in graduate studies must change.[33] But first-year writing faculty often face even more detached relationships with composition studies, and addressing this fact is important as we rethink other parts of the profession.

As I illustrated in the previous chapter, the traditional prewrite/write/rewrite model has been one of the major methods through which the intellectual and disciplinary matters of composition studies have been repressed and upon which opportunities for the participation and contributions of many members of the writing classes have been suppressed. Before moving to a description of the process through which my colleagues and I have begun to challenge these limitations, it is important to remember that the course happens in the context of using invention, arrangement, and revision to open the field back out to teachers and students. Analyzing these elements reintroduces reading as one activity through which it is possible to learn something about writing—and about written discourse—without sacrificing a focus on process to some misplaced notion of texts as the gods of what needs to be said, explicated, and reproduced. To help readers remember that this is the context within which the rest of the course occurs, and to remind readers that analysis of invention, arrangement, and revision positions students to enter conversations in new ways even in classes where the teacher is not focusing on those issues, my students and I have decided that I should present some individual student analyses of invention, arrangement, and revision before describing the course. I will, therefore, present two individual analyses of invention, arrangement, and revision. Remember, these analyses are starting points for discussing reading and writing. They create grounds for discussions that allow teachers to see students' analyses as opening spaces for reading and writing. We are considering the questions: What is invention? What's being invented? What is arrangement? What's being arranged? What is revision? What's being revised?

In the article discussed in this response, William A. Diehl and Larry Mikulecky explore "one of the roles of reading instruction receiving increased attention . . . , that of preparing individuals for the literacy demands of occupations" (371). We often read this article (or one like it) early in the semester to both broaden our basis for understanding literacy as an area of study and to enrich the ways we can reflect upon the relationships between our own literacy histories and our expanding literacy needs. Teachers' focuses for exploring the discipline can also emerge from this activity, especially when readings about occupational matters and the issue of identification (see second analysis below) are raised early in the course.

ANALYSIS ONE
Jennifer Hartenbower's Analysis of
"The Nature of Reading at Work"

Invention

What Is Invention?

had to have knowledge and understanding of "functional" job literacy
need to have read and analyzed the research of others in the field of
    reading at work
understand the way literacy is taught and assessed in school and for jobs
understand the four categories of strategies used in reading for work
see and analyze the difference between school and work literacy

What Is Being Invented?

a new way of looking at literacy in the work place
show that there is a difference in the level of literacy required for school
    and work
understanding of how much more helpful it is to have the readings in
    context with actual physical processes
show that there is error in the way that required literacy levels in the
    work place are being assessed

Arrangement

What Is Arrangement?

whole to part
division into the two sections of job reading and school reading
inclusion of the research of other experts on the subject
use of sample situations to reinforce the ideas of reading in association
    with a physical activity

What Is Being Arranged?

"representative" literacy tasks vs. real-life literacy tasks
job-related literacy in comparison to school literacy
literacy demands vs. literacy availability
job reading tasks vs. school reading tasks
reading comprehension in relation to cracking the code
read-to-learn as opposed to read-to-do
reading with information-rich context as opposed to reading in isola-
    tion

Revision

What Is Revision?

the use of whole to part arrangement

the use of hypothetical situations to illustrate points

the paragraph about the majority of job reading is required daily or at least once a week

the several references to the idea that more research needs to be done in this field.

What Is Being Revised?

the idea that one's reading comprehension in isolation does not necessarily show the persons ability to do a job accurately

the notion that more research needs to be done in this field

the difference between on-the-job reading and school/training reading situations

change the way literacy is assessed in the work place

the idea that maybe schools are not appropriately preparing students to be functionally literate

In chapter two of *Hunger of Memory*, Richard Rodriguez discusses the ways that his education separated him from his parents and, eventually, brought him to a place where he could understand and challenge the terms upon which that separation was based. We often read this selection (or others like it) early in the semester. Analyzing this type of text allows us to explore the ways that identification with often informs our literacy histories in significant ways and to begin building conceptual frames that open alternative routes to literate subjectivity.

ANALYSIS 2
Amanda Hamilton's analysis of "Chapter 2" of
The Hunger of Memory

Invention

What Is Invention?

secondary research

research and review of published materials-uses many ideas from another published work (Hoggart's *The Uses of Literacy*)

gives detailed background information

lists credentials (Ph.D.) and schools he graduated from

lists his own published works

uses definitions of "scholarship boy" to describe himself and other students

What Is Being Invented?

idea that individuals must eventually leave their comfort zones to learn and understand new knowledge and participate socially

idea that students deemed "scholarship boys" experience success because of their special anxiety to learn

definition of "scholarship boy" – good student, troubled son

idea that working-class citizens' lifestyles are different than the ways children learn in school

idea that there will be a separation between the student and his parents

idea that parents will powerfully measure the changes in their children after they attend school

idea that parents will be supportive and give up so much so that their children can be successful

idea that parents want more for their children, want better chances, than what they had

idea that a person should always try to better himself (and his family), whether educationally, spiritually, or financially

idea that with an education one can do anything he sets his mind to

idea that teachers are knowledgeable, confident, and authoritative

idea that a reader needs to feel camaraderie and communication with a writer

idea that theme gives a book its value

idea that "scholarship boys" are mimics, do not think for themselves, and do not form their own opinions

idea that students with such an eager desire to learn only imitate others' opinions

Arrangement

What Is Arrangement?

uses ideas filled with irony – what he was expressing was actually different than what he was feeling

uses dialogue to recap parts of conversations from his past

uses flashback

uses quotes from published materials

uses repetition of what it means to be a "scholarship boy"

What Is Being Arranged?

his success is being put in relation to his resulting loss

he compares himself as the "scholarship boy" in relation to the fourteen year old girl in the classroom – both anxious to learn

when student sees his parents, he is reminded of the person he used to be

old way of life that has been lost is put in relation to new life that has educational benefits

the experience of growing up and becoming educated is put in relation to the idea that many people share the common experience of education so they can enter the world

borrowed ideas of a "scholarship boy" are put in relation to original ideas of other individuals

Revision

What Is Revision?

uses long quotations to interest readers

produces many ideas about education

creates a feeling of emptiness in becoming obsessed with learning

shares many personal experiences to capture readers

influences readers with personal feelings and beliefs

What Is Being Revised?

idea that adjusting from childhood habits to a classroom environment is difficult only for working-class children

idea that one can succeed without receiving help from others and without having determination and persistence

idea that an individual can forget information or situations by trying to forget them

idea that reading all the time makes an individual a good reader

idea that "scholarship boys" are good students

idea that schools change students too much

As we discuss these analyses in class and work toward shared understandings of the relationships between and among invention, arrangement, and revision within and across our analyses, we are able to broaden our ideas of writing, of form/content relationships, and the repertoire of strategies available to us as we use language to make meaning of and in our own processes and products. Using the analyses to look across texts of the same type (for example, literacy histories) and across texts of different types (for example literacy histories and scholarship about the history of literacy in the west), invites us to begin understanding the ways that invention, arrangement and revision are engaged in different, complementary, and similar ways according to rhetorical situations and purposes. As I have discussed at length in previous chapters, we do so not only to identify these strategies, but also to develop an understanding of the ways that student writers are and are not invited to see this rich spectrum of possibilities as available to them and to understand the challenges of moving past the limited notions of these activities that we bring with us to our writing classrooms and writing activities. The collaborations, cross-class activities, reading, writing, and community literacy activities that accompany this work happen in the context of these discussions.

DEFINING SHARED COURSE FOCUSES AND SELECTING COURSE MATERIALS

Obviously, individual sections of any class in a first-year writing sequence must take into account the larger curricular goals for that course, the relationship between those goals and other courses in the sequence (should they exist), and the various other contexts within which learners will be expected to apply the knowledge they have gained in that class. Encouraging faculty to work together to create individual sections of a first-semester course in ways that allow students and faculty to work across sections is not always easy. Too often, requiring a shared textbook or reader takes the place of collaborative work that allows for cross-class activities. To address this problem, and to begin making transitions that would help us overcome the ways that first-year writing classes are structured as isolated spaces, I worked with my colleagues

Bonnie Gunzenhauser and Rosemarie King-Grindy to create syllabi around shared and complementary activities. Selecting what will be shared across sections and what will be selected to complement work across sections is an important part of challenging the literacy boundaries that have become naturalized in our introductions to composition studies. While those boundaries may be constructed differently at different institutions, thereby requiring different responses, it is important to attempt these crossings if we are to change the ground of first-year writing. I offer an outline of the ways we decided to create approaches to first-semester writing based on a shared and complementary approach not to prescribe the product of our work, but to clarify the issues that arise as important when we attempt this kind of border crossing.

We began with a clear sense that moving away from the prewrite/write/rewrite models informing our initial introductions to teaching first-year writing had been critical in our work as teachers. We knew that using the concepts of invention, arrangement, and revision would be one of the shared components of our classes because they had helped us begin to see the ways that the course might be redefined as a place where students and faculty could practice participation and contribution. In our own process of working together, it had become clear that being able to talk across texts, experiences, and areas of expertise had enriched our understanding of literacy in significant ways, so we decided to find ways to allow that to happen across our sections of the course. This would allow students to write to one another about what we were studying without requiring them to use the same texts. In addition, it would have the effect of foregrounding the writing issues we were studying; students could write to one another about the relationship between the invention, arrangement, and revision activities and the content of the essays. Having shared components in the formal writing assignments would also allow students to read across their formal texts in similar ways. In both cases, students would be building a knowledge base that, in practice, invited them to understand writing and reading as dynamic processes that can have significant effects on our relationships to the discipline and to the world.

COLLABORATIONS

Many layers of collaborative work inform the approach to composition studies that I put forth here. As discussed above, cross-class work is one important layer of constituting composition studies as a collaborative endeavor in which different members of the writing classes can participate and contribute. In class, students also write formal and informal texts collaboratively. Community literacy collaborations are one way to make this happen. Not all schools and/or faculty are in a position to engage in such work, however, and that should not be seen as a detriment to other kinds of collaborative work that can help to position participation and contribution as vital to composition studies. Collaboration between and among faculty colleagues who create curricula, syllabi, assignments, lists of readings, and other activities that cross traditional class boundaries can also have positive effects, even when community-based literacy work is not possible. Working together to identify these opportunities in specific institutional contexts can become part of the work of faculty members who teach the course. It is not enough to create shared goals for a curriculum, we must do so in ways that construct participation and contribution as important to the teaching of writing and to the departments in which that teaching occurs.

My colleagues and I have also written grants to support our work, focusing early on grants that would give us time to read together about the history of reading in the West, the history of composition studies, the teaching of research, and texts from each of our areas of expertise that related to those issues. We have presented together on campus and at a variety of conferences, and we have created syllabi, assignments, and other classroom materials collaboratively. Students from these courses and I have also collaborated, sometimes while they were in the course but more often after they have finished the class and begun projects of their own. We have revised course materials, presented on campus and at conferences, and supported one another in a variety of writing projects. I suspect that many people who teach first-year writing are engaged in similar activities, but that those activities remain disconnected from their conceptions of composition studies. As we begin to bring these activities into view through new work or descriptions of current work, we must simultaneously revise our ideas about the discipline if we are to value them in more general ways (more about this in chapter five).

In the conversation that follows, Bonnie, Rosemarie, and I discuss how our work together has affected our teaching, research, scholarship, and service; I have encouraged these faculty, and many others, to think about these components of their professional lives in integrated ways. Both my current institution and my introduction to service-learning through a colleague and Illinois Campus Compact helped me to work toward a view of administering first-year writing programs in ways that encourage the integration of teaching, research, scholarship, and service to enhance faculty development, improve the program, and revise the profession. I will present our conversation without interruption to illustrate some of the ways that our work together helped to produce more integrated ideas about and experiences of the field. Our conversations took place in my home during a two-hour recorded session.[34]

Nancy: How has our collaboration affected your ideas about composition studies and the teaching of first-year writing?

Rosemarie: I had never thought about reading as much as I have since we started doing this. I always assumed that students didn't really know how to read, but this has given me tools to help them learn how to be good critical, rhetorical readers. In a way I have always felt like I was sort of floundering, and now there's this nice concrete model that works not just for reading but also for the teaching of the writing too. I would just sort of go through the text and say here's the things I want to call attention to rather than saying you need to look at every piece of writing that is something we have written, not something that magically appeared. But this [invention, arrangement, and revision] has given me a vocabulary, ideas about how to approach that much more efficiently than I've done before.

Nancy: Did you use pre-writing?

Rosemarie: I've never done pre-writing except when I was in graduate
school, and you had to. And I did my requisite composition theory courses, and we learned about these various
things. I really never did fit into that. I did it for my man-
datory one semester and then did my own thing after
that.

Bonnie: I would agree about the fact that a big part of the value
of this collaboration for me has been finding a way to
connect reading and writing more fruitfully. The idea
that using literature to teach composition is not particularly effective—that was not a new idea to me. The kind
of composition training I have had was reader-response
based. Readers expect this, and so as a writer it's your
job to understand those expectations and to construct
documents in ways that fulfill those expectations, which I
actually don't dislike and I think it makes a lot of sense.
But I think it assumes a pretty high degree of competency
already for the writer. And, I think that when you're
teaching first-year composition you can't assume that level
of sophistication. And, I think it's part of our job to
cultivate a higher level of sophistication. And so using
reading so as not just to give students ideas to engage
with, but as a way to look at texts as written documents constructed for a variety of purposes, using a
variety of methods or invention strategies, has been
really invaluable as a way of integrating the contents of
the course in a way so that reading and writing function
together as a way of bringing students to greater sophistication as readers and as writers.

Rosemarie: And as thinkers.

Bonnie: Yes, as thinkers.

Nancy: For me the invention, arrangement, and revision strategies came first; I started using that in class. Starting to
understand what it meant to pick texts that made that
as effective as possible was a slower process and a much
more collaborative process because, of course, that really
came together when we started working together. When

we first did the joint lectures I remember thinking that the three pieces [of our work] are also things we should be thinking about when picking readings for the course. I knew I wanted non-fiction that we could look at writers as well as readers, but it was really hard—especially before it was about literacy and I just sort of picked these random things from popular culture or whatever.

How have invention, arrangement, and revision affected your ideas about composition studies, if at all?

Bonnie: That assumes I had a lot of ideas about composition studies beforehand.

Nancy: But, if you didn't have a lot and now you do, I want to talk about that too. And if you don't have any more than you did before that, it's fine too. I'm just wondering, especially since our work has moved you both into presenting about the teaching of writing.

Bonnie: Our collaboration has made me aware in a way I was not aware before of all the odd ways that people go about teaching first-year writing—the fact that it's often the course that people feel has been foisted upon them. It's a course where people try to shoe-horn in their own interests at the expense of attending responsibly to cultivating good reading and writing skills in their students. That's not just to be critical. I think that most of the people who teach composition don't have much understanding of composition studies or composition theory. It's just a thing they end up doing. Part of the reason, I think, the . . . strategies work so well is because they are very portable. And, I think part of the reason we've been able to collaborate so well is we're each very different in our intellectual orientation and our scholarly orientation. But, like Rosemary was saying, invention, arrangement, and revision give us a common vocabulary that we can use when looking at almost any text or set of texts. And so, it seems to me that one key thing for composition studies is coming up with some kind of analytic vocabulary that allows people from a whole variety of perspectives to participate and teach responsibly. And in a way that has intellectual content as far as being connected to course readings. That, I think, is the big difference because most people could probably say something about I cluster, I brainstorm, I free-write, and I teach my students to do that. And then they write a paper, and I have them read each other's paper, and then they revise. And so, I'm teaching them a responsible kind of process. And, that's O.K., but ideally you can teach them both a responsible process and, like Rosemary was saying earlier, help them to become more sophisticated thinkers as far as engaging the texts and ideas and the kinds of things they presumably came to college to engage in.

Rosemarie: The way that we try to do our course really encourages students to see the relevance of reading and writing in their lives in ways that the standard English 101 and 102 classes don't. Because we have invention, arrangement, and revision, because we start with them and stay with them and evolve over the course of the semester, it becomes a tool students carry out beyond our class. In contrast, the classes I've seen and even been forced to teach on occasion, which are okay, now we're doing the narrative, now we're doing the this kind—never the twain shall meet kind of thing – students don't really see how it has any effect except now I know how to write this kind of paper. And another thing, the reading that a lot of students do in those other kinds of classes is [to say if they] agree or disagree and why—a kind of dualistic way of thinking is encouraged rather than discouraged, I see frequently. And I think we're great. I think we're doing a good job of trying to get them to avoid that kind of thing and to look at things in different ways instead of the either/or mentality, which couldn't be more timely.

Nancy: Some of the materials are about people who have had very different literacy issues than our students have had, and sometimes not as different as we imagine, and so any kind of approach that elicits judgment before it asks people to think about these differences can be very mean.

Rosemarie: I don't know how often it happens at our school, but I
            know at another school among some of the teachers,
            there's almost no reading that goes on in the first semes-
            ter. Students are asked to write argument papers, and
            they have little or no knowledge of what they're supposed
            to be writing about. And, again, having a schematic or
            focus on literacy as a topic really helps because they do
            get some knowledge of a particular area that has some
            depth and some complexity and lots of different angles,
            and that's a really valuable thing for them to see they
            have to have substance behind what they're saying. And,
            I don't always see that to the degree that it needs to be
            seen because it's coming out of a certain model of com-
            position teaching that is that sort of free-writing, rewriting
            kind of thing. It just encourages not just all sorts of bad
            habits but also a dangerous way of looking at the world, I
            think.

Bonnie: It's interesting. I think the literacy has worked well for us
            as a focus, but I know that in my experience it has worked
            better as a focus when the students are doing service
            learning than when they aren't. Because, yes I think our
            course helps them to see the importance of reading and
            writing in their lives, but I also think that unless they're
            seeing at play in their work with people who have real live
            problems with literacy issues, by about November, they
            feel like, Oh, my God, reading and writing—it's enough
            already.

Nancy: If they're not doing the service learning, they feel that
            way. It's just a topic. I haven't done it without the service
            learning.

Bonnie: I have been forced to, and people said that to me and
            they said that in course evaluations. It made a big differ-
            ence.

Rosemarie: And, it did for me, too, on the semesters—one or two
            years—I was paired with two different cohorts. In the
            one we were going up to Clinton and doing that, and the
            other one was doing something completely different. And
            in one semester, in particular, that was problematic for

the students. The other time I did it, it was a group that was—just by luck—interested enough in the topic, and we did the gen-X stuff and got into that. It is harder—service learning makes a big difference. I think you're right. It really does help to pull things together.

Nancy: Has our work together affected your research? I know it has affected our service work at our university.

Bonnie: It's affected my research in that—in my own research before I ever started doing this—I was interested in the social function of reading and writing in the Romantic period. And, when I came here, teaching composition was half of my load, and it's nice to find a way to integrate half of your teaching load with your scholarly life. And, so, having a way to think theoretically and collaboratively – a way to teach composition that was helping our students understand the potential social power of reading and writing, or the power of literate action, was great for me. It allowed me to think of what I was doing as all kind of a piece. And when we did the grant together, and when we read those books together, and when we did our evening lecture event, we developed a common ground for understanding what we're doing. So I think more than the isolated presentations we've done—just the way it's allowed me internally to integrate my sense of what I'm up to as a teacher and researcher has been probably the biggest thing for me.

Rosemarie: Obviously my research interests aren't that explicitly connected. But obviously literacy issues have a whole lot to do with what's going on in South Africa, with Gordimer's audience. I just don't read things the same way as I did before. And I find myself making those kinds of connections and being more critical of her as a result of the work we've done here. Access to materials and things like that . . . the socio-political and the social class out of which she's coming and those kind of things have been in the foreground of my thinking more than they were before we started doing this. The students just love the lecture that we do together, and one of the things that's

really neat about it is it does show them here are three
people with very different interests, but whose work is all
connected to literacy in some way. That's really useful.

Bonnie: For me, it might be the only place in the course where I
actually can come clean about my real area of expertise
and what it is. And so, having something good in the
first semester of their first year, where people actually do
come clean about their real intellectual interests and say,
"Look, this connects to what we're doing in this class and
you can, too"—I think it's a good model for them. And
I think some of the assignments we use—like that reflective paper where we ask them to think about how their
literacy history has changed and how that might play out
in their own career choice or future life choices, invites
them to do the same thing—to think about how this fits
into their actual intellectual lives and not just how—now
they have their "A" and they can go on their way and get
down to the real business. I think that's good—great!

Nancy: You said something that made me remember all that
reading we did together—especially for the grant—
because like the Gordimer stuff about writing, and listening to Rosemary's work, has made me read some more
of *Writing Being.* Not only has that influenced my scholarship, but also how I'm able to be in the classroom and the
kinds of things I'm able to refer to. The same with the
18th century literacy movement work that Bonnie does.
That has been really eye-opening—partly because I had 2
courses in 18th century rhetoric. We don't look at any of
that stuff. You don't look at Hannah Moore. I never even
heard her name. And that seems to me a really important person for somebody who's studying the history
of writing. It gives you a whole new perspective on why
Campbell, Blair, and Whatley got as popular as they did.
Gaps in my knowledge base have been addressed through
our work together, but it hasn't made me feel like, "Oh,
my God, I don't know what I'm doing." To get introduced
to new stuff and not feel threatened by your lack of
knowledge of the historical context and the really deep

roots of what you have been missing is something that is really interesting to me. And it's something I think about more generally in class. You know, when we do the hooks stuff, students will say, "Oh, she's just saying everything is white people's problems. And this is just about white man's guilt." It's easier for me to respond now. I'm much less defensive because of our work together.

Bonnie: I think ideally that's what collaboration does. It allows you to augment your knowledge base without feeling like an idiot for not knowing the things you didn't know.

Nancy: That's really the stuff I had for us to talk about. We talked about it affecting teaching and scholarship. I have also service—university service and community service at our disposal. Obviously the community literacy stuff is a big way that it's affected all of our service activities. Anything else?

Bonnie: I think the lecture is the something else.

Nancy: The lecture—that's been interesting. You both talk about the lecture a lot.

Bonnie: I think lecture aside, the biggest thing, for me, has been that when you're at a small teaching institution, you're always going to be the only person in your field. And so, if you're going to have any kind of collective, intellectual life at your institution, it's going to have to come through collaborative efforts that bridge gaps across different fields. And, I think first-year writing is a really natural place for that to happen because so many people teach it. And, I think that one thing this collaboration has accomplished and shown me is that there are ways to collaborate that are both true to the aims of teaching what first-year writing should be about and that make room for intellectual interests that might not explicitly seem to be very connected at all to issues in composition studies. But that, in fact, can be connected without gluing things together in an artificial way.

As our conversation illustrates, teaching first-year writing can be an alienating experience when faculty feel there is no connection between the ways they have been taught to teach those courses and the values that drive their ideas about English studies.[35] The split between reading and writing is at the heart of this dilemma, but methods that simplify issues such as genre, audience, the relevance of literacy in various contexts, and the relationship between the courses and their knowledge about other aspects of English studies also interrupted participants' ability to think about participation and contribution as vital to their work in this area. Our collaborative grant work, the development of shared and complementary approaches to course design, building bridges across our individual areas of expertise by reading and writing across those differences, lecturing and presenting together, and creating a shared ground for reflection helped us to get past the histories that had interrupted the possibilities for collaborative participation and contribution in our lives as first-year writing teachers, and as researchers and scholars.

CROSS-CLASS WORK

Working across the class boundaries that usually define composition courses can also help us make transitions that invite members of the writing classes to view writing within the larger literacy contexts informing people's lives and to understand the possibilities of literate action. These crossings may seem less significant than those I will discuss in the next section when I talk about our community literacy work. But they are equally important to creating a community of people—teachers and students—who explore, define, and communicate about disciplinary matters in ways that challenge habits that create and maintain the class structures of higher education. We cross these boundaries in a number of ways.

For example, curricula based on shared and complementary readings allow us to work together to create contextualized views of literacy. Using the shared invention, arrangement, and revision questions and the shared readings, learners from one section of the course can write to those in other sections about complementary materials. When we are reading literacy histories, readers of hooks' *Remembered Rapture* and readers of Welty's *One Writer's Beginnings* can write to one another about how the texts deal with our shared focuses for study. (Whether communication occurs electronically or in hard-copy form depends upon what resources are available, what the participants prefer, etc. Participants can discuss the issue and set criteria for decision-making. These kinds of discussions often open interesting questions about technology and literacy.)

Students also do cross-class peer critiques of first and/or second versions of their own papers. (Again, participants can decide how they want to exchange papers. I have rolling file cabinets outside my office door. Each student in each participating section has a folder in the cart so that there is a central drop-off and pick-up place for exchanges of hard-copy versions of written work. If schedules allow, teachers can exchange sets of papers and deliver them in class.) Readers can use the shared invention, arrangement, and revision questions to read each other's texts. Other issues and questions writers would like readers to address, and those that have grown from our analyses can be added to peer reading guides. For example, at some point in our analyses, issues of format, font and other visual components of invention, arrangement, and/or revision will become important. Issues about audience always arise from our analyses, as do issues of style, access to information, etc. We address these issues as they arise. Sometimes it takes students a little while to get used to the idea that their texts will be read in the same way as other course materials; they are used to their work being responded to in very different ways than are the other texts informing their educational situations. Challenging this assumption also invites discussions about the place of writing—in this case student writing—in the larger literacy contexts informing our lives, and creates ways to reflect upon how related assumptions limit the possibilities for literate action. As is often the case, the quality of peer critiques varies greatly, although having common issues that students address as readers and writers has, in general, increased our ability to focus on the form/content relationship at the level of process. It has helped me to see and experience the ways in which merely reading student texts or placing them at the center of first-year writing does not necessarily change the ground of and for composition studies. It has also opened new disciplinary conversations with colleagues at my home institution and at other institutions.

Other cross-class activities have involved students research-ing and writing across sections of the course, faculty lectures that address students from different classes (this has been espe-cially true across honors sections of the course), faculty projects like designing shared and complementary curricula, presenting together about the work at conferences, and the planning of joint writing ventures.

COMMUNITY BASED LITERACY WORK

As part of their course requirements, students tutor for one hour per week in community literacy classes that I have helped my community partner, Project READ, move onto our campus. Three types of courses are held on campus: general education (GED) classes, English as a second language (ESL) classes and Adult Basic Education (ABE) classes. Before classes were held on campus, the west side of Decatur did not have a place to hold community lit-eracy classes. Because the other major site for such courses is quite far from the west side, because many of the students who drop out of high school attended school on the west side, and because our site is more accessible via public transportation, creating this site was important for a number of reasons. There is, of course, a long history behind the reality that creates a situation in which students can now tutor on campus rather than being transported to other sites. (The first semester I had students tutor as part of course requirements they went to four different sites—and so did I.) And there is a long history to why working with a community literacy partner and its constituencies is a course requirement. In relation to the goals under discussion here—opening spaces for contribu-tion and participation and the activities that can help us make that transition, i.e. viewing writing within the larger contexts of literacy and opening possibilities for literate action—the requirement serves two main purposes. First, it configures present experiences that bear on the writing issues being composed through first-year composition classes. Second, as a result, it focuses our work in ways that allow for a dialectic relationship between past and current experience, between known and new knowledge, between learning from and contributing to our study of writing.

Students in these sections of first-year writing and GED students start the semester by writing their own literacy histories and sharing what they discover through exploring their own literacy educations. The university students will have attended in-class training sessions run by our community partner agency. At training sessions, Millikin students will be oriented toward the multi-dimensional view of literacy (e.g., family literacy, computer literacy, math literacy and so on) used by that organization as well as beginning their tutor training. Obviously readings connected to these forms of literacy and/or readings that address those issues in some way will be important during the time students are receiving their training.

FORMAL WRITING ASSIGNMENTS

Because the approach to composition being outlined here aims at helping the members of the writing classes make transitions that open spaces for participation and contribution, there is, in some ways, a high level of similarity between the kinds of assignments made popular in first-phase process movement pedagogies and those put forth in the revisions I suggest here. One of these similarities is that the initial assignment is strongly connected to experience (although this scene includes personal experiences of people other than the individual writer in the isolated composition class). Another is that each assignment focuses on writing as a process (although in this scene students explore writing as a process rather than enact a particular version of it). There are also differences, however, because the assignments are constructed to foster approaches that open spaces for participation and contribution. Therefore, assignments follow a pattern established as important to that goal. Our first semester course is called Critical Writing, Reading, and Research. Contextualizing the personal, considering the historical context of a subject, considering the cultural context of a subject, putting one's understanding of these things in relation to relevant disciplinary contexts and discussions, and reflecting in ways that make one's new understanding of a subject in light of those activities are critical endeavors that accommodate many disciplinary formations of what it means to be prepared to participate in and contribute to, rather than merely consume, a discipline.

The first paper, then, is an exploration of the relationships between literacy and experience that invites investigations of the social, familial, and educational factors that affect those relationships. Obviously, individuals will have different experiences, and creating a picture of those differences across individual student papers should be a significant activity once those papers are completed. That is, the papers are not graded and left behind, but become texts to read together in ways that add something to what we can know about reading and writing. In this way, students are engaged in creating knowledge about some of the same things members of the profession are interested in developing knowledge about. Putting these two bodies of knowledge in relationship to one another becomes possible through this activity.

Paper two is an exploration of some historical aspect of literacy that becomes important during the first formal assignment. Again, this is an important area of research in composition studies and opens another opportunity to put the field and student discourses in relationship with one another. The papers can be integrated into the course as texts that help us understand the similarities and differences between and among the ways that historical contexts relate to current literacy developments.

Paper three is designed to give us a chance to understand the cultural contexts that affect, but are often transparent in, our literacy lives. Many faculty move to popular culture to create a frame for this assignment. Obviously, there are many ways in which our professional discourses are concerned about these issues. Consequently, we create further ground upon which these two usually separated spheres for creating understanding might speak and listen to one another in enriching ways.

Paper four is a deep exploration of how first-year writing students are constructed in disciplinary conversations within composition studies. We create texts that use our literacy histories and other course materials to respond to those constructions. Our goal is to create responses that will be relevant to the field and to explore the barriers to and possibilities for getting access to professional forums. Course readings, experiences as community literacy tutors, relevant personal experiences and/or the knowledge developed through analysis of student papers are put in relation to disciplinary issues that individual students think deserve further attention. In this assignment, students practice participating by offering new relevant focuses for those of us who construct their lives as members of our writing classes.

Paper five is a revised literacy history that focuses upon ways to integrate the knowledge we have developed over the semester into the literacy lives of individuals, our future goals, the program, the experiences of future participants, and the teaching of first-semester writing more generally. The integration of new knowledge into these arenas is, of course, part of the work of professionals in the field as well, creating further opportunities for connection-making and collaboration across these discourses. We cannot set aside the fact that the course is often students' only introduction to the kinds of writing that they will be expected to do throughout their time in higher education. We also must remember that many people who teach the course have been using a modes and/or aims-based approach that favors beginning the semester with a personal narrative, and that the approach has much to recommend it if we are going to invite faculty and students to contribute to and participate in composition studies. As I said earlier, however, making the transition to courses focused on participation and contribution requires the creation of a new context for writing; changing one element of the situation and leaving all others the same has not resulted in changing the material and/or ideological positions of most members of the writing classes. All of the assignments work toward helping us view writing within the larger literacy contexts informing people's lives and creating an environment within which those views reflect the possibilities of literate activity. There is no assumed split here between the history of composition studies and these goals. It would, in fact, be impossible for me to argue that experience, theory, or the practice of teaching and learning within first-phase process model movement assumptions did not inform the ways students and others invited me to create the approach to composition put forth here. While identification with those assumptions is not the only, or even primary, feature of that relationship, other kinds of relationships with that history and its materials—counter-identification, resistance, and even rejection—are an intimate part of the work. In fact, if we limit writing to identificatory activities, we simply can't begin to understand participation and contribution as vital to composition studies. Before discussing in more detail the particular ways that formal writing assignments occur in these attempts to open spaces for participation and contribution to become defining features of the disciplinary practices of first-year writing, let me note that it would be possible to discuss the same sequence of assignments in relation to different goals—for example, consumption of a particular rendition of writing as a process, or as adaptation to some normalized set of linguistic expectations or assumptions about audience. The academic context within which writing assignments occur is at least as important as is any other rhetorical situation they are expected to address, especially when the two situations accompany one another but are different in significant ways. Here, formal writing assignments exist in relation to explorations that put writing in relation to a variety of literacy contexts for the purpose of understanding and challenging the ways that the possibilities for literate action are defined within those contexts.

The first assignment of the course works toward the goal of viewing writing within the literacy contexts informing people's lives by asking students—first-year writing students at the university and students in the GED class we'll tutor in—to write literacy histories. Millikin students will have read a variety of literacy histories by this point in the semester; GED students will have been introduced to a fairly traditional notion of prewriting (e.g., brainstorming, clustering, etc.) and will be working on prewriting activities with a tutor from the course. The course tutors will introduce the GED students to other invention strategies that we have seen at work in our own literacy autobiographies and in our other readings. Asking questions of adults who might remember literacy events in the students' lives, creating metaphors for explaining literacy, defining literacy in relation to unusual language events, etc. are all strategies that university students might share as ways for GED students to think about getting ready to write their essays. Because GED students are preparing for a timed essay (50 minutes long), they tend to favor strategies they can use in that timed situation, and so do we. GED students come with the expectation that they will receive writing instruction from a university professor (me) and will have tutors who have agreed to foreground their goal of passing the exam. When tutors have extra time to spend with students, they focus on studying for other parts of the exam (e.g. social studies, science, grammar and usage, math) with the GED students as has been promised. University students often know lots of strategies for taking timed essay exams that our GED students can really benefit from practicing, and students often spend lots of time discussing these strategies, especially those that help improve reading speed and comprehension. The first assignment, then, helps all constituents understand how writing is positioned and positions students in different ways according to the expectations put forth and the evaluation criteria and assessment practices that will be used even as it invites students to explore their individual literacy histories. Overt discussions about the ways that these assumptions and practices define possibilities for literate action take place in university and GED classrooms. This activity continues throughout the semester, and is the focus for university students' community literacy journals. ESL and ABE issues are also addressed in course readings and discussions; students tutoring in those classes keep track of how what we are learning in class does and does not transfer into those situations.

The second formal writing assignment creates a context for understanding the importance of historical studies in literacy situations that favor participation and contribution. We read texts about some historical aspect of literacy that surfaced as significant in our literacy histories. We analyze the invention, arrangement, and revision activities in historical texts and begin to develop an understanding of the differences in these strategies within and across different kinds of texts (e.g., the historical texts and the literacy autobiographies). Writing assignments focus on integration of historical contexts and the affects of that integration on our abilities to understand ourselves and our lives as literate human beings in new ways and on the process of coming to see how that new understanding might be significant to larger discussions about literacy.

The third formal writing assignment invites students to explore and practice alternative literacy strategies. This assignment introduces students to the ways considering cultural contexts affects our understanding in general, and on the ways cultural studies informs composition studies in particular. It is designed to help us begin to understand how more traditionally critical approaches help us view the literacy contexts informing people's lives. Readings might include a reversal essay like Horace Miner's "Body Rituals Among the Nacirema," or a piece of science fiction that creates an alternative world that comments on reality in some way (e.g. *Herland*). The goal here is to open a discussion about how critique reflects a view of the world that calls for literacy paradigms that are not restricted by the assumption that identification of is always or necessarily just a precursor to identification with. Readings illustrate ways that writers engage invention, arrangement, and revision strategies when their purpose is to invite something other than identification with their subject. At this stage of the course, we explore literate subjectivity as being composed through and in complex ways that can call up responses other than identification with and that, therefore, may indicate needs and activities that would not otherwise come into view. University students practice using some of the invention, arrangement, and revision strategies they identified in the readings and/or others that they create. GED students are working on an essay that asks them to identify a problem in their neighborhood and pose solutions for that problem (a common prompt on the exam). Each group is engaged in literacy activities that call for identification of (the structure of a set of cultural artifacts or a neighborhood problem, for example) without prescribing identification with (the cultural products are critiqued and the problem is responded to rather than described). In other words, this work helps us understand negative responses, refusals, rejections, problem/solution formats etc. as literate activities.

The fourth formal writing assignment helps us to use our own course of study to make a contribution for some specific purpose. The project is sometimes a collaborative piece both within and across sections of the course. Often, our Project READ partners enter the conversation, attending classes to talk about how the community literacy work is going and to help give focus to our work. Readings and particular writing assignments are determined according to project needs. Recently, for example, Project READ staff needed to write an extra grant because of state funding cuts. After discussing the matter with them, it was decided that members of two sections of the course would meet with a variety of students in the GED, ESL, and Adult Basic Education courses to tape their literacy histories. Tapes were then transcribed by university students and became part of the grant. Students in other sections 1) worked with the director and staff of Project READ to create a history of that organization and 2) did research to update information about the populations served by that organization. Other projects have included research and the creation of documents to improve retention in Project READ courses, research and proposals that clarified the computer literacy needs of the GED part of the program, the creation of public service announcements, and book drives. Oftentimes this project requires the use of a variety of kinds of technology, tape recorders, cameras, web research, online library research, etc. We discuss all of the technologies we use in relation to the invention, arrangement, and revision activities we gain access to through these technologies and as a result of their availability. In addition to these issues, collaborative work focused in this way allows us to begin to understand what it means to use literacy for projects that include members of populations with very different histories, starting places, ideas about needs and so on and to struggle together to act in ways that respect these difference as we work toward defining and reaching a common goal.

One other activity is also occurring at this time and, in fact, in recent revisions to the course assignment sequence, this activity is becoming central. At this point in the semester, students are also reading texts about first-year writing students. They are analyzing those texts, especially the ways those texts construct first-year writers, so that we may make overt the differences between those constructions of student writers and student writing and the actual student writers and student texts in the class. The texts students produce about these matters relate directly to a significant disciplinary conversation they can contribute to in real ways.

In earlier versions of this curriculum, the fourth assignment was a deep exploration of the ways that we can use a variety of kinds of knowledge—experience, imagination, various forms of primary and secondary research as well as various kinds of invention and arrangement strategies—to center revision in our composing processes. Some of my colleagues and I found Virginia Woolf's *A Room of One's Own* a good way to open conversations about revision at this point in the course, and to move students toward a deeper understanding of the study of writing. The book makes the relationships between and among the six questions about invention, arrangement, and revision clear, and it does so in ways that invite reflection upon the historical, critical, and collaborative literacy contexts explored earlier in the semester. Students would write a formal stream of consciousness paper, exploring the relationship between literacy and some chosen second term (Woolf's text explores the relationships between women and fiction and money and space). Over the course of writing this paper, conversations about integrating new knowledge about a subject, in this case literacy, in ways that inform our scholarly lives and our lives more generally became prominent. Understanding the ways that thinking about invention, arrangement, and revision as readers and as writers invites learners to become participants in the conversations informing the pedagogies that define the material realities of their status as members of the writing classes is also a common conversation when this assignment is employed. GED students will be working on a 200– to 250–word essay that also asks them to write about a relationship so that conversations about the writing issues connected to that process are primary for all of the writers who are working together.

For the final formal assignment, students create revised literacy histories. This focus on revision gives us lots of time to reflect on the knowledge about literacy that we have consumed and produced over the course of our time together, and to focus on how that knowledge revises our insights into our literacy pasts, our current literacy situations, and our ideas of ourselves as teachers and learners. Students choose and/or create new invention, arrangement, and revision strategies for this assignment. Together we all focus on the ways that becoming members of the composition class who use knowledge and experience to contribute to as well as consume the knowledge bases that preceded our participation requires different activities than those usually required of us in educational settings. Students are encouraged to put their work in relation to some other area or areas of their lives as learners. Many put their work in relation to their growing literacy needs in their chosen discipline, in higher education more generally, or in relation to the needs of their families or other community groups they are involved with.

As is the case in many programs, this first-semester course is followed by a second-semester course focused on developing the skills, knowledge building, and attitudes that foster engaged critical research informed by a strong sense of purpose. Students who have been introduced to the concepts of invention, arrangement, and revision can apply those concepts as readers who can analyze the discursive patterns across the texts they read for their research projects. For example, recently a student who was researching gender patterns in communication between college-age men and women who are romantically involved for the purpose of improving communication among members in that group noticed that discourses about this subject in popular publications and those in academic publications were significantly different. Analyzing invention, arrangement, and revision uncovered not only textual feature differences, but differences in the assumptions and purposes informing these two types of discourses about the same things. For example, the popular texts tended to discuss gender differences as essential and unchangeable while the academic sources tended to discuss gender as socially constructed and more flexible (especially across class and sexual preference). The purpose of the popular texts was often to give advice, while the academic sources often took challenging assumptions as their purpose. When this student turned to writing, she decided to use invention, arrangement, and revision strategies from both sets of texts to illustrate the ways that her audience members needed to see both the benefits of researching issues that they tended to see as naturalized and the importance of changing attitudes and behaviors as a result of that knowledge. She was able to meet her own purpose of helping romantically involved heterosexual college students communicate more effectively by helping them identify their assumptions about and purposes for communication in their relationships. She was also able to indicate some attitudinal and behavioral changes they could use to improve communication. She did primary research to identify the major concerns men and women had about their communication problems with romantic partners so that she could organize her text in ways that would engage readers early on and connect the materials she understood as important in this conversation to her readers' concerns.

Because invention, arrangement, and revision can function as both analytic and generative concepts and activities, students and faculty can move toward more integrated experiences as readers and writers across literacy situations. As grounds for analysis, these concepts invite readers to understand the relationship between form and content in new ways, and to develop increasingly sophisticated ideas about the expectations for participation and contribution. As generative practices, invention, arrangement, and revision allow writers to make decisions based upon their knowledge of these expectations without restricting them to the replication of textual features they see at work in any one text or genre. Students find that participating in and contributing to the conversations informing their research about a variety of topics often requires them to make overt the limited perspectives that shape the texts in which they ground their research. While not all students make inclusion of a new perspective the purpose of their research papers, they all do come to understand that contributing to the conversations that construct the assumptions and realities upon which our lives are based is an important activity.

Within this assignment sequence, invention, arrangement, and revision can also operate as analytic and generative concepts for faculty teaching in the program. We have analyzed the differences between and among the patterns of invention, arrangement, and revision in published research, in research textbooks, and in student papers. Our analyses have allowed us to generate course goals and materials that do not confine us to status-quo assumptions about student research. We have been able to develop approaches to the second-semester course that make understanding those status-quo assumptions a critical activity for all of the members of our writing classes. Because the prewrite/write/rewrite model is too focused on prescribing certain sets of activities, it cannot help us to develop critical literacy in these ways. Using invention, arrangement, and revision as analytic and generative concepts sets the ground for making transitions toward practices that invite all members of the writing classes to participate in and contribute to composition studies, and to configure participation and contribution as vital components of literacy more generally.

CONCLUSION

I have described the ways that colleagues and I have begun to open spaces for participation and contribution not to prescribe those particular practices (which change as new faculty join our efforts and as student contributions redefine our work), but to suggest how opening these spaces led us to question the isolationist view of curriculum design that limited our potential as teachers and scholars in the same ways it limited the potential of our students. Collaboration, cross-class work, and assignments that put student discourses and the discourses of the discipline in relationships with one another became possible as we moved away from the traditional prewrite/write/rewrite notion of process. These activities may prove effective across institutional settings. In any case, moving from prewrite/write/rewrite to invention, arrangement, and revision calls up different ways of centering participation and contribution as vital to composition studies.

5
REVISING ENGLISH STUDIES

Throughout this book, I have been arguing against assumptions and practices that preclude students and many teachers from participating in and contributing to composition studies. As I conclude, I would like to put these matters in relation to contemporary discussions of the theory/teaching split that some see as defining the next generation of composition studies. I will draw heavily from two collections of essays that are often cited as central in contemporary attempts to chart new directions for composition studies: the 1997 collection *Composition in the Twenty-First Century: Crisis and Change* edited by Lynn Z. Bloom, Donald Daiker, and Edward M. White and the 2002 collection *Rhetoric and Composition as Intellectual Work* edited by Gary Olson. My discussion will illustrate how repositioning all members of the writing classes as able to participate in and contribute to composition studies requires a reversal of the common assumption that transformation of the field occurs from the "top" down. In that rendition of the field theorists and experts introduce new concepts and practices that filter down through instructional materials to teachers and students who are expected to identify with the assumptions behind those materials even though, in most cases, they are not familiar with those materials. In addition, when those materials hold out different activities for the teachers and students of composition studies than theorists had to engage in to create the work, this scenario constructs further distance between and among the members of writing classes and their texts. This double negation of the possibilities for participation and contribution—the neglect that comes from restricting access to materials that define the lives of literate human beings and of posing that neglect as necessary to the life of a field of study so intimately connected with the constitution of that literacy—creates limited and limiting subject positions for many members of the writing classes even in discussions about how the field is—or should be—changing.

Conversations about changing the field tend to move in two seemingly contradictory directions. They either focus on the ways that rhetoric and composition must move away from its concern with teaching—and especially the teaching of first-year writing—to develop its "intellectual" potential or on the ways that classroom practices must remain disconnected from this or that set of theoretical matters in a quest to empower students. Oddly enough, although these conversations seem to be at odds with one another, they are, in some ways based upon similar concerns and absences. Their shared concerns include:

1) A new focus on the texts that will inform the practices of the field
2) A concern about the place of first-year writing (whether first-year writing is seen as a positive or negative part of the field).

Both conversations also fail to overtly address:

1) The valorization of practices that continue to position the majority of people who are in the field and their discourses as absent from its forums
2) The absence of conversations about the ways that first-year writing might be a place where we could actively engage many of the larger social concerns our field claims to be worried about—the inclusion of voices from previously ignored and/or repressed people and points of view, writing subjectivity and agency, and consciousness.

But arguments that ignore these similarities and pretend that the healthy intellectual life of the field hangs in the balance as we decide which side of the theory/practice split to valorize play a bit too much like "reality" TV: there's lots of manufactured drama, and it takes the place of reality. If it is true, as Linda Flower asserts, that "composition courses reflect our public visions of literacy," they do so largely without the input or response of the majority of people who teach and learn in composition classrooms (249). This is partly because in the society of composition studies "it is not unusual to find a department, at least in large universities, where the faculty teaches only majors and graduate students" (Bartholomae 20). In fact, at conferences I have heard statistics that indicate that as many as 80% of the people who are awarded the Ph. D. in Rhetoric and Composition never teach first-year writing after they leave graduate school. All of these conditions defer the real problems associated with creating more inclusive theoretical and practical realities within the profession. Like the manufactured drama of "reality" TV, the manufactured drama about the importance of choosing either theory or practice, either intellectual endeavors or teaching, covers over the fact that reality exists somewhere outside of that drama—in thousands of undergraduate first-year composition classes taught by thousands of people who are considered less a part of the field than people who do not teach first-year writing (many of whom are directing programs) and even more thousands of students who are considered even less a part of the field than are their teachers. The "vision" of literacy that emerges within these realities is, of necessity, hierarchical and elitist: people must climb up and away from the lower classes to be granted the privilege of participation and contribution. Like "reality" TV this construction of the discipline favors games about who gets excluded, voted out, if you will. That the thing being dismissed created the upper classes that either no longer need or want this history is not an issue in approaches that posit theory and practice as separate. (Who really believes that we would have faculty positions in graduate programs if we did not have undergraduate writing courses, especially first-year writing courses?) More important, this restriction of the literate subjectivities of the members of those lower classes is not considered a significant loss to the profession, probably because the majority of people in those classes were never really considered to be in the field to begin with. As Anne Ruggles Gere notes in "The Long Revolution in Composition," versions of these contradictions have been embraced by the field "over the past three decades" (120). And while I do not agree with Gere's reading of Susan Miller's *Textual Carnivals* (120), I do agree that "the contests and oppositions evident in [the] varying ways of thinking about student identities only suggests the many new concepts of humans . . . have emerged in composition studies during the past couple of decades" (121). Invoking Lester Faigley, Gere insists "theories and metaphors" of subjectivity that inform composition theories and practices "must begin from the premise that student identities cannot be defined as stable or unified"

(121). Of course, student identities can be—and often have been—defined in these ways, but this is beside the point. The real question here is: What does it mean that a field so strongly informed by attempts to establish its own stability as a discipline and to assert its place as necessary to the unity of English studies denies these forms of identity, especially at specific developmental stages—to a majority of the members of that field? What are the implications of defining student identities as unstable, especially in relationship to the discourses students are asked to produce and the ways those discourses are and are not included in the disciplinary structures of the spaces that make up the field? As Trimbur notes, the ways we have organized the field and

> attempted to expand what it means to do scholarship by arguing why and how teaching composition, administering programs, and writing textbooks can and should be counted as scholarly activities, at least when done properly, [are] . . . normal moves to establish codes of practice, bodies of scholarship, and general professional standards . . . to determine what counts as a contribution. (135)

As Trimbur further notes, these normalizing activities and the "professional formations" (137–38) and "stratifications" (138–140) they create "reproduce the logic of professionalization by assuming that "entering the conversation" depends on personal acts of will, individual expertise, and career building" (140). Trimbur ends his essay by stating "We need . . . to develop new ways to read the contradictions of professional life, to grapple daily with the persistent conflicts between building individual careers and popularizing expertise for broader social purposes" (145). Clearly, students, and many teachers will have little to no agency in such a professional scene if their discourses are not included in the professional spaces upon which the field bases its assumptions about these matters. If participation and contribution do not define the relationships between and among the diverse members who constitute the field and the field, we cannot hope to challenge these conflicts and contradictions or to replace them with conflicts and contradictions that are more inclusive. What is at stake in this argument is not whether theory or practice is more important to the intellectual life of the discipline, but whether the discourses of diverse people in the discipline are important to the discipline. Centering the theory-practice split as *the* scholarly business about which the discipline argues and through which it creates camps does not help us to open spaces within which the participation and contributions of many members of the field can come to define the field. No matter which side of the argument one favors, the argument itself does not address the segregation of discourses upon which the field is currently based. It is a mistake, I think, to continue down any path—theoretical or pedagogical—that assumes we can create social spaces through composition studies that we are not creating in composition studies.

In her review of *Rhetoric and Composition as Intellectual Work,* Elizabeth Flynn notes that conversations about the "importance of rhetoric and composition as intellectual work . . . insist on the continued development of the field as an agent for change" (981). But in many ways the agency referred to here belongs primarily to a sub-set of the members of the field. For the essays in the collection do not discuss students as active participants in this change process, even though serious redefinitions of student subjectivity are at issue in many of the essays in the collection.[36] It is within this frame that Gary Olson proposes that we separate the "intellectuals" from the "anti-intellectuals," with intellectuals defined as people who "do" theory that does not "constitute rhetoric and composition as a discipline whose raison d'être is the teaching of writing" (24) and anti-intellectuals as people who constitute rhetoric and composition in this way. Olson asserts that what "distressed some compositionists" about this particular rendition of the intellectual/anti-intellectual, theory/practice split was

> that the field was no longer defined simply as self-reflection about the teaching of writing or about one's own (or one's students') writing practices, [for] while it included these concerns, composition had become much more expansive, encompassing broad and diverse investigations of how written discourse works. (23)

Setting aside Olson's literal simplification of the movements' earlier reflections about writing and teaching, and even ignoring the historical inaccuracy of his assertion that such reflections had not come from and led to "broad and diverse investigations of how written discourse works", we are still left with the fact that he dramatizes people's reactions as "distress" rather than commitment to something that cannot be accommodated in the binarized configuration of the field he conjures up. He ignores the fact that the "expansions" he refers to are not so easily disconnected from the teaching of writing and its concerns. The real limitations of this argument are revealed, however, when Olson defends himself against Wendy Bishop's charge that he is "intentionally not interested" in "inviting eighteen-year-olds to enter the sentence" that he writes about the pedagogical scene of which they are a part.[37] That someone might challenge the fact that the students are part of the scene he is discussing but not part of his audience "mystifies" Olson. He states:

> I certainly did not intend that prose for eighteen-year-olds. For a quarter of a century, I've been teaching that good writing is all about addressing a particular audience for a particular reason. Why in the world would I want undergraduates to "enter" a piece that is explicitly about composition "scholarship"? The audience is the undergraduate's teacher. She [Bishop] cites Toby Fulwiler, who similarly complains that the "exclusionary use of language" by the discourse community of composition scholars "makes it difficult for eighteen-year-olds to enter and participate" (Fulwiler 220). . . . Since when is scholarship in any field written with undergraduates in mind? Do we have to certify that nuclear physicists write in such a way that sophomores can "enter and participate" in their scholarly discussions? Surely there is a serious confusion here between the goals of and audiences for *scholarly* writing and the goals of and audiences for other types of writing. (27)

The use of a scientific model for scholarship is invoked here without any reference to the critiques of that model that inform the serious intellectual, theoretical, and pedagogical discussions of the first-phase process movement and subsequent critiques of the scientism some see as informing the cognitive bases of that movement.[38] Bishop and Fulwiler aren't arguing that composition and science are or should be the same, or that student subjectivity is or should be constructed through the same set of disciplinary practices across different disciplines. They are making an argument for the creation of real connections between beliefs about the power of literacy and the constitution of literate subject positions for members of a discipline. This critique has a strong history of and commitment to the relationship between literacy and the possibility for active participation in the constitution of one's material realities.

Olson's configuration of the history of composition studies allows him to ignore the fact that writing "with undergraduates in mind" is, and has been, a serious matter in writing studies because it challenges the very traditional ideas about audience—and about self/other relationships more generally—that he puts forth here. According to Olson, people can be talked about and/or the experiences that define their existences in material ways (in this case their educational experiences in composition classrooms) can be discussed and constructed without consideration of their understanding or participation. This practice comes dangerously close to reinscribing a kind of colonizing approach to constructing the relationship between the subjects of a discourse (i.e. composition students and teachers) and the role that discourse plays in the constitution of their material realities. That is, the argument for a view of rhetoric and composition that does not define "all research, all theory, all scholarship" as existing "for the sole purpose of furthering and refining the *teaching* of composition," raises serious issues about and challenges to the ways such "scholarly work" positions members of the writing classes in relation to one another's discourses. The assumption that discourse has to be written specifically for undergraduates to be understood by undergraduates is an extreme illustration of the way that the split between theory and practice—and the split between reading and writing—is based on and maintains limited subject positions for many of the members of the writing classes. And although Olson chooses to interpret challenges to these sorts of configurations of self/other relationships among members of our discipline as "backlash against theoretical scholarship" (14, 24), some of these challenges, including my own, are something altogether different. For many of us, the assertion that any one mode of discourse (in this case theory) can or should define what counts as "intellectual" work is too ironically anti-intellectual to be comfortable. We have studied the many different ways that many kinds of discourses can be understood to contain deep intellectual content. In fact, this insight was one of the realizations that came from the expanding notions of discourse and how it works that Olson had claimed for his own argument earlier in the essay. The assertion that one kind of discourse should be held up as *the* form within which intelligence springs forth and/or can be expressed ignores both the history of composition's struggle to move away from the limitations of that conception (especially in relation to explication) and the very real ways that such a conception of discourse limits what knowledge is. The knowledge/intelligence split that drives this conception of theory simply replicates the use of discourse as a tool for regulating access to our field's public forums. But the more important issue here is identified by Carla Leah Hood in her response to Scott Mclemee's article "Deconstructing Composition: The New Theory Wars Break Out in an Unlikely Discipline," which appeared in the March 21, 2003 issue of *The Chronicle of Higher Education.* Hood states:

> One of the crucial features of the controversy that composition has inspired is absent from [this] article: the disconnection between what is considered content in first-year composition courses and what are considered composition texts in the field. In other words, students are required to take composition to learn the conventions of academic writing; they are not required to take composition to learn the field of composition. If any aspect of composition needs to be deconstructed, it is this one. (B17)

The idea that students "are required to take composition to learn the conventions of academic writing" (as if this could happen without access to the ways that participation and contribution define academic writing practices) erases the theoretical, pedagogical, and embodied history of composition studies in particular and of higher education in America more generally. It means that students do not have to read composition studies to be "in" composition studies, and that what they do learn about the field is superfluous to their lives as writers and readers. (No one would argue that history is not a necessary type of discourse in history classes, or that philosophy is not a necessary type of discourse in philosophy classes, etc.) But the fact that this erasure is based upon a split between "what is considered content in first-year composition courses and what are considered composition texts in the field" is accurate. Bridging this gap is not only a matter of bringing the materials of composition studies into the first-year writing classroom, however. It is, instead, a more serious matter that requires us to confront the ideologies, theories, and practices through which we constitute self/other relationships in the field. In other words, understood as the historical institutional justification for the accommodation of theory, or as the material reality that opens the space of composition studies outward to the study of literacy more generally, or as the material space within which all of the members of the writing classes can gain access to the field, or as the activity upon which composition studies revisions disciplinarity and the traditional hierarchies of the academy, the teaching of writing is not—and never has been—only about teaching as teaching is configured in Olson's argument. More important, perhaps, the space for theory claimed by the argument, the idea that writing theory does not emerge from and can not or does not exist in relation to teaching (and other institutional matters) is misguided. Even the theory that is produced by academics who do not teach or who do not wish to address pedagogical matters does have something to do with teaching, insofar as others are doing the teaching that funds the institutional structures from which that theory emerges. In addition, even when it does not define teaching as its subject, theories that emerge from work done in the academy do get taught and do affect how and what teaching gets done. One is drawn again to the similarities between this view of teaching, institutional power relationships, and theory as a type of discourse that is somehow disconnected from the business of academia and the type of reality represented on reality TV. In this scene, if theory doesn't take affecting teaching as its purpose, then theory gets to pretend it is disconnected from any of the relationships that connect it to the material practices and spaces upon which it depends for its existence, and anybody who doesn't go along with the pretense doesn't get to play the game.

In "Coming to Terms: Theory, Writing, Politics," an essay that appears later in the same collection, Lynn Worsham notes that the theory-practice split is a result of the traditional ways that composition studies has become professionalized.

> In short, composition, like literary studies, has become an institution, one that is more rather than less closed off from the larger social world in which it is situated by its own insular and professional disputes—the most consequential being the ongoing battle over the nature of "our" work. This dispute—often abbreviated as the theory-practice split—involves those who maintain that the field's proper work must remain strictly limited to the teaching of writing and the research required for that project, and those who insist that the scope of composition includes anything that bears on literacy, broadly conceived, and the workings of written discourse. . . . I suggest that if we persist in allowing the "theory-practice split" to govern the social relations of the field—and ultimately the way we articulate our role in the university and its relation to society—then we do so because we prefer to misperceive the nature of the task at hand: we must make the academic work of composition studies more vigorously, more resolutely intellectual.
>
> The sine qua non of intellectual work is theory; thus the primary way to make the work of composition more seriously intellectual is to make it more seriously theoretical. . . . What we must do . . . is to understand, and to make explicit, the profoundly rhetorical (and political) nature of theory. (102–3)

It matters, of course, who "we" are here. And in a sense, this is the issue I have been addressing throughout the book. For what is the position of different people's discourses in the field if, as Worsham indicates in her conclusion, "we truly value work directed toward effecting social and political change" and if, as she continues, "it is incumbent on us as intellectuals to continue the 'deadly serious' work of making 'really free' places, lives, and identities"[39] (112). Who, exactly is doing the making here? Who is being placed in the position of being made? Furthermore, can this sort of metaphor for manufacturing freedom—where some make free "places," "lives" and "identities" for the rest of us—work? What is freedom in this structural configuration of who creates and who is created for/on? Where are the spaces within which freedom could be a result of the assumptions at work here? And if this freedom is made for spaces outside of those within which it is manufactured rather than inside those spaces, if it is assumed that the world can change even as the profession stays the same, then are professional spaces justifiable? Obviously, I am worried that the field is being too strongly constituted as the kind of space that ignores these questions. One of the main reasons I have this worry is because of our tendency to favor metaphors of transformation over transition. In her conclusion to *Composition in the Twenty-First Century: Crisis and Change,* Lynn Z. Bloom states her concern about these metaphors of transformation:

> If there is a conspicuous gap in *Composition in the 21ˢᵗ Century,* other than its rather slight concern with the liberatory and textual power of creative writing, it is the indifference to the economics of these various visions of disciplinary and consequent social reform. . . .
>
> If the profession cannot ensure the funding for its broad-based, unsettled, unsettling, and undoubtedly expensive agenda, what chance is there not only for reformation of the status quo but also for the utter transformation that Flower, Gere, Trimbur, Heath, and Lunsford, among others, envision? (276)

These expenses are not merely economic, although Bloom is right to worry over that aspect, as any of us who have been doing the kinds of work discussed here can attest to. Mostly, I have come to understand that self/other relationships are constrained by systems that define participation and contribution in ways that close these activities off to certain members of the writing classes. I suspect that this has happened partly because a rhetoric of participation and contribution would require us to revise the very notion of situatedness that underlies most of the rhetoric of the field. In such a rhetorical scene, where rhetoric not only gives us audiences, but also makes us audiences, we would have to attend equally to what kinds of audiences our rhetorics make us as we do to what kinds of writers they make us and the majority of members of writing classes. If my rhetoric requires my audiences to stay in suppressed positions as writers, then I can easily deny those writers access to the forums in which I discuss them and/or their texts with other audiences. Once part of a population is excluded in these ways, it's not as hard to substitute opportunities other than participation and contribution as adequate practices for rhetors and audiences alike. We have, I think, become a certain kind of audience for student discourses, one that needs only a certain type of student texts: those that can be considered irrelevant to our professional lives except as objects through which we construct assessment rubrics, textbooks, justifications for our existence, and arguments about what kinds of discourse should and should not be considered worthy of inclusion in our professional spaces once student discourse has been bracketed from those spaces.

Over the past year, I have been fortunate to consult with Bob Broad as the faculty in my department work toward new forms of assessment.[40] As we read student texts together in small groups, faculty members concentrated on naming what we valued in a series of student texts. In those sessions, facilitators Carmella Braniger, Michael George and myself worked hard to keep ourselves and our colleagues focused on what we valued in and about those texts. We all had to make an effort to move out of our conceptions of ourselves as certain kinds of readers of and audiences for student discourses to be able to discuss what we valued about those discourses. Moving away from reading student discourse only to identify problems and weaknesses and to make academic evaluative judgments is important, however, if we want to see the value of including those discourses in composition studies as we revise curricula and set new grounds for participation and contribution. Our work has indicated some serious gaps between what we value in first semester students' texts and the stated goals for the first-semester course, gaps that are inevitable when goals are set to standards that assume very limited roles for those texts outside of the classroom and very traditional evaluative practices. In "Literate Action," Linda Flower describes an undergraduate class in which students work with "inner-city teenagers" to produce a newsletter and a "public Community Conversation" about some public issue relevant to the teenagers' lives. At the start of the article Flower states:

> Traditionally, the academy has wrapped itself in the cloak of what Deborah Brandt calls textual literacy, idealizing the autonomous text and valorizing the essayistic mind. . . . Expressivist literacy, on the other hand, according to John Willinsky, embraces self-discovery and an aesthetic of craft and creativity. More recently, a third vision, which we might call rhetorical literacy, is emerging as the social, the cognitive and the rhetorical strands of English studies weave themselves together and begin another reconstruction of composition. Rhetorical literacy revolves around literate action. In place of a decontextualized, logically, and linguistically autonomous text, rhetorical literacy places a writer—a rhetor, if you will—as an agent within a social and rhetorical context. (249)

Flower is not discussing a first-year writing class here. But as I have discussed previously, and as others have shown, the introduction of community literacy activities operates to expose the differences between and among rhetorical contexts—those of academia and those of a community literacy agency, for example—in many of the ways the article outlines.[41] What is disturbing here is that the academic context is positioned as arhetorical rather than as a rhetorical context with its own sets of expectations, discursive conventions, purposes, and configurations of writing subjectivity and audience. As we know, even many of our first-year writing students and teachers do not understand the traditional academic context as arhetorical, but as restricted by rhetorical conventions and expectations that create a form of discourse that has no place in the discipline from which it draws its subject matter and emerges. And while I agree that we must continue to seek alternative forums for student discourses, I do not agree that doing so can or should take the place of creating spaces for those discourses within the field of composition studies itself. In fact, the relationship between those we include and those we do not, and the ways our theories and practices open and close spaces for participation and contribution, may be the defining relationship upon which possibilities for transition and transformation rest in our disciplinary conversations and structures. How we respond to the problem of the inequities fostered by systems of literacy in which some people are only or primarily talked about and/or to (with little attention given to their ideas about how they are being talked about and/or to or to their own ideas about the issues surrounding those discourses) may have a special importance to us if the transformations we desire are at all possible. Transitional spaces, practices, pedagogies, theories, and professional behaviors may be necessary to overcoming these inequities. How these transitions are enacted, if they work, is more than a matter of if people whose voices haven't previously had a forum now write things "worth" inclusion in our professional publications. We can't simply say that if they were good enough they would be there, for certainly if first-year writing students were or felt invited to submit to those publications their numbers alone would ensure some sort of representation. In this new rhetoric, it matters what we do as audiences for the massive amounts of student texts that we ask people to produce and which we read. (I am not in favor of doing away with student writing as a strategy for dealing with these problems.) The myth of "the Rhetor," like the myth of "The Author," as an individual who is solely responsible for whether a text is persuasive must be seriously challenged for new ways of creating self/other relationships to become possible. We must continue to explore and address the ways in which we, as audiences, hold certain assumptions about a certain genre—student discourses—and certain writers—students—to challenge the limitations placed on that genre and those people by our assumptions. What students are taught or not taught about composition studies, what kinds of papers they do and do not write, how strongly those papers are constructed as isolated events disconnected from other discourses about the same things, and where they are and are not allowed or invited to go has, I think, too much to do with what they are and are not like for us to ignore these issues any longer.

What I have been suggesting here is that participation and contribution are vital concepts as we explore these issues and attempt to create transitional practices within which enriched and enriching subject positions become available to the lower classes in composition studies. If those practices open spaces outside of the field—in community agencies, for example—and not inside the field, we should not accept that as enough. At the very least, we should begin from the belief that composition studies is capable of opening spaces for all members of the writing classes to participate in and contribute to the discourses that define their material realities as members of those classes.

EPILOGUE

As I am finishing this book, I am also working with five colleagues to create a sequence of assignments for our first-semester "Critical Writing, Reading, and Research" course. To support our work, we wrote a proposal for an institutional grant, and we were awarded compensation to meet together for one week. To prepare, each of us read about some aspect of literacy to present to the group. Carmella J. Braniger has just finished her first year of teaching at Millikin University; she chose to explore orality as her literacy issue. Michael W. George has been on the faculty at Millikin for two years; he chose to explore technological literacy. Paul Haspel has just finished his first year of teaching at Millikin; he chose to explore visual literacy. Greg Sullivan has also just finished his first year at Millikin; he chose reading as his focus for our work together. Each of us chose a literacy issue that both connected to previous areas of interest and needed to be thought through in relation to first-year writing. I prepared and presented about recent discussions of the relationship between assignment writing and assessment. Focusing on literacy issues of interest to individuals allowed each of us to pick an area we were really interested in, and to explore it in relation to reading and writing. The bibliographies that people created from their research included texts by scholars in composition studies as a matter of course. No one prompted others to look specifically for work by scholars in the field, but one can't really get too deep into any literacy issue without encountering that work. Often, one of us would find a source that related to another person's focus area, and we would share that information. This collaborative sharing of scholarly work helped people see the connections between and among the areas of literacy we were focused on. As we were working, I realized that this is why I had chosen the topic of literacy some eight years ago when I decided that bringing composition studies into my composition classrooms was a vital step in my life as a teacher, learner, and administrator in the field. Focusing on literacy in development activities with first-year writing faculty puts people from across English studies in relationship with the discourses of composition studies. The process had not so much directed people to texts in the field as it had illustrated the importance of those texts in explorations of a variety of literacy issues. We can have confidence about this matter as we revise composition studies to include the discourses of the field.

After each person in the group presented her or his research, we began to create a sequence of assignments that would allow critical writing, reading, and, to a lesser extent, critical research to become the subject matter of our first-semester composition classrooms. We developed an outline for a sequence of assignments that we will use to create drafts of each of the assignments. Our goal is to create formal assignments that are flexible enough to accommodate shared and complementary readings that enrich cross-class activities. The first assignment will be a literacy history. Students will read and think about a variety of ways people write about the history of literacy, and they will compose their own literacy history. The second assignment will invite students to read, think, and write about some form of literacy they are unfamiliar with; it is my belief that there should be some historical component to the study of literacy connected to this assignment. The issue of the importance of historical work has caused the most resistance from members of the group. The third assignment will focus on the exploration of some everyday artifact not previously considered by the author in a critical way. Here we will introduce critical analytic and generative strategies for dealing with popular artifacts. The fourth assignment will invite students to read, think, and write about the constructions of themselves as literate human beings in articles about first-year writers and writing. They will write papers that add to the conversations about themselves that inform composition studies. The fifth paper will be a revised literacy history. These are general outlines for the assignments, literally being constructed as I write this epilogue. Each major assignment of the semester will introduce some scholarship from composition studies into the course. Our work has already helped me to clarify the ways that the personal, historical, cultural, disciplinary, and reflective can be discussed in faculty development forums as vital components of critical literacy that open spaces for participation and contribution to teachers and students. We have not yet decided upon exact readings for each section (remember some will be shared readings across sections and other will be complementary so students can write across sections to one another about different readings about the same issue), but our grant work has clearly illustrated the importance of composition studies to the lives of teachers and students in the field.

We have decided that all faculty will use the invention, arrangement, and revision concepts I have discussed throughout this book as analytic activities and generative practices throughout the semester. Students and faculty will be talking and writing together about the ways that literacy, and the study of literacy, enriches the knowledge bases they can draw from as they make decisions about invention, arrangement, and revision as writers. And they will be actively engaged in moving to practice as writers, teachers, and learners from those new knowledge bases. In this way, composition studies is informed by the richness of the literacy histories of all of its members, and it can, therefore take the enrichment of the literacy lives of the members of the disciple as its purpose in new ways.

NOTES

1. According to Parks, the arguments that created a more conservative view of writing teacher were successful in part because "they cast '60s teachers' as naive" (217). As I will illustrate in chapter three, similar arguments are used by people who cast process teachers as naive in their attempts to position "post-process" theory as the best ground for contemporary composition studies.

2. Parks uses Donald Murray's "Finding Your Own Voice: Teaching Composition in the Age of Dissent," and his "Teach Writing as Process Not Product" among others to show how Murray's arguments repress what the student writing of the Free Speech Movement illustrates students do know about political discourse so that a picture of the student as a depoliticized subject can emerge as central to the teaching of writing. Parks explains:

    > Having ignored the actual political content of the first Free Speech Movement, and given the perceived lack of "legitimate" political discussion occurring, Murray (1969) argues that students need to learn what free speech and political speech imply. (Any sampling of the actual extended documents produced by the Free Speech Movement would have demonstrated a knowledge of legitimate political discussion by the participants). (79)

    This allows Murray, and others, to position teaching students the correct, "legitimate" way to write political discourse as something that must precede their engagement in political discourse, and discourse about political issues more generally.

    When combined with Murray's skewed picture of the student power movement as resting upon "rhetoric that is crude, vigorous, usually uninformed, frequently obscene, and often threatening," an agenda for the writing classroom emerges; the teacher must fight this rhetoric with workshops on "civic responsibility" that begin from the false assumption that student power comes from and will assume such "crude" discursive practices unless it is contained by the lessons about free speech and political speech that students are taught in the writing classroom (79). Parks goes on to illustrate the ways that this approach to the teaching of writing and the assumptions upon which it rests must construct students as individuals with their own voices whose individuality and power are obstructed—rather than enriched—by their lives as members of communities with shared language patterns and practices. Ultimately, Parks argues, in approaches based upon these assumptions, "the writing classroom becomes the cutting edge of activism *by* teachers" (85). For students in this scenario "politics becomes personal liberation, not the dynamics of group organization toward a political goal" (86). Organization toward goals—and the definition of goals themselves—are the business of teachers.

3. The details of North's proposal can be found in his book.

4. This book is written using many of the invention, arrangement, and revision concepts and strategies developed from the same approach to engaging process discussed in chapter three.

CHAPTER ONE

5. For an approach that suggests that we begin classes by asking students about their ideas concerning what good writing is, see Ira Shor's *Empowering Education: Critical Teaching for Social Change.*

6. I explore the suppression of our experiences in writing classrooms at length in "I Was a Process-Model Baby."

7. We have, I think, been better at addressing writing in the discipline issues outside of our profession than within our profession.

8. See "Reconfiguring the Grounds of/for Composition: Alternative Routes to Subjectivity in the Work of James A. Berlin."

9. For an early extended discussion of the ways that first-year writing has been constructed to favor mastery see chapters 5, 6, and 7 in Richard Ohmann's *English in America: A Radical View of the Profession.*" For a different, but equally compelling view of the ways that modernism challenged the mastery narrative surrounding literacy see Raymond Williams *"Writing in Society."*

10. For an extended discussion of the ways that selecting and reading texts that start from very different assumptions about rhetorical matters than those informing first-phase process models, see Jacqueline Jones Royster's "*Traces of a Stream: Literacy and Social Change Among African American Women.*"

11. Travis is a computer science major and a writing minor; he will graduate in the spring of 2004.

12. Starting next year the students in my Critical Writing, Reading and Researching I classes will engage in the kind of analysis the student consultants helped me develop here. Student consultants included: Linda Osborne is a forty-five year old English Literature major who has long-standing interests in class issues and in lesbian theory, fiction, and practices. She describes herself as a radical lesbian socialist feminist. I first met her when her advisor suggested that she talk with me about ways to understand the codes of higher education at work in her new environment when she transferred to Millikin after finishing her Associates Degree at the local community college; she graduated with her Bachelor's degree in May of 2003. Jennifer Eason is a traditional age student whose primary interest has been creative writing. Although not an English Education major, she was a teaching assistant in a first semester Critical Writing, Reading and Research (IN 150) course in the fall of 2002 (many of our students who are considering going to graduate school spend a semester working with a professor of that course). Jennifer graduated in 2003. Kathy Klemesrud has been both a political science major and an English major. She is a currently a political science major with a writing minor, and will graduate in May of 2004. Kathy is interested in drama, as a playwright, as a theorist, and as a rhetorician; she is also interested in entertainment law. Meg Schleppenbach is an English Education major who has also been a teaching assistant in IN 150. She will attend graduate school in an Education department next year. Her primary interests concern secondary education in America, especially the ways that that system fails large portions of our population and how we might go about making real improvements. Nicole Cassidy is a junior English Writing major with a Spanish minor; she is interested in English as a Second Language and is planning a

career in that field. As I write, she is in the Dominican Republic for a semester abroad. Carrie Owens is an English Secondary Education major who is interested in beginning her career as a high school teacher upon graduating in spring of 2003; she has been a teaching assistant in IN 150. I met with these students in two groups on subsequent days to accommodate their schedules. Carrie, Meg, Kathy, Travis and I met together on the first day; Linda, Jennifer, Travis and I met together on the second day. Both sessions were taped and subsequently transcribed by my generous colleague, Dianne Devore, who teaches one of the GED classes that my students and I tutor in each year.

13. See Murray's "Writing as Process: How Writing Finds Its Own Meaning." Early in the essay, Murray states: "The process of making meaning with written language can not be understood by looking backward from a finished page" (3). This assertion is questionable on a number of levels. Most important are the questions that arise when the reader of that page is the writer of that page and questions regarding the restrictive notions of analysis implied about reading here. In the first case, the writer is blocked from entering disciplinary discussions about process; in the second case, reading is clearly not analytic or critical. As I explained in my introduction, Murray's assertions rest on a particular notion of the student as being in need of freedom from others ideas, discourses, etc.

14. Krista Ratcliffe's work about rhetorical listening promises to add much to our conversations about how to deal with these issues in the classroom.

15. As Royster Notes in *Traces of a Stream*, rhetorical action does not take adaptation as its primary goal.

> To focus on the kaleidoscope related to rhetorical action, African American women transform the world they perceive into the worlds they desire through the use of language. In the space between the perceived world and the desired worlds is a hermeneutic problem space, in which there are opportunities for individual writers to use language in a variety of literate acts: making problems visible, clarifying and amplifying imperatives; establishing more useful terministic screens or interpretive lenses; maintaining a sense of mutual interest or common ground;

negotiating and mediating differences. All these literate acts can be categorized as participating variously in the creation of a consubstantial space for the conversion or subversion of interests, for the affirmation of new horizons, and for the facilitation of change in attitude, behavior, or belief. (70–71)

CHAPTER TWO

16. By 1994, of course, theory and theorizing were being positioned more generally as the new center of English studies. Even a cursory look at the scholarship of rhetoric and composition from that period will illustrate how much of that same theory was also being favored by literary studies.

17. More recently, of course, theory is positioned by some as not only a corrective, but also as the thing we lost as the profession became focused on process and more inclusive practices, and as the loss that has squelched the intellectual existence of composition studies and those who teach it. In "Reclaiming Our Theoretical Heritage: A Big Fish Tale," for example, Jasper Neel states: "By 1950, we had lost our theory of being, and then we lost both our cultural justification and our reason for being" (10). In an essay with no references to the feminist theory of the time, to the theoretical work behind the process movement of the time, in fact, no citations from any texts by women as far as I can tell, Neel asserts the loss of theory. The alternative theories of the fifties, for example feminism and the theories informing and emerging from the civil rights movement, are ignored here as challenges to the "theory of being" and the methods of theorizing about "being" Neel reengages in his essay. Ultimately, then, the question is who is the "we" Neel refers to here as losing their theory of being, cultural justification, and reason for being?

18. I realize that this is not the usual profile of first-year writing teachers. See Helmers 139–148 and Miller "Feminization" for other discussions of the image of the theoretically challenged first-year writing teacher.

19. This alternative story is not so much a fiction as a repressed narrative.

CHAPTER THREE

20. We read the chapter about advanced placement courses from Richard Ohmann's *English in America* at the point at which these issues arise in the classroom.

21. This is true no matter what kind of first-year writing class I am teaching, honors classes, "regular" sections of the course, or classes for under-prepared students.

22. I have taught basic writing courses in the university very infrequently as my current institution has not historically had separate classes for students who need more individual help, choosing instead to attach a one-hour individual tutoring session to students' schedules as necessary.

23. For extended discussions of the ways that arrangement has been conflated to matters of textual form, see Berlin, Crowley, and Jarrett.

24. Ellen Cushman makes a similar observation in "The Rhetorician as an Agent of Social Change" where she states:

> I am not asking for composition teachers to march into homes, churches, community centers, and schools of their communities. I'm not asking for us to become social workers either. I am asking for a deeper consideration of the civic purpose of our *positions* in the academy, of what we do with our knowledge, for whom, and by what means. I am asking for a shift in our critical focus away from our own navels, Madonna, and cereal boxes to the ways in which we can begin to locate ourselves within the democratic process of everyday teaching and learning in our neighborhoods. (12)

25. I would like to thank my nephew Peter DeJoy for helping me find a new way to merge my introduction of the place of children's literature and its role in defining literate subjectivity. Peter introduced me to Doreen Cronin and Betsy Lewin's *Click, Clack, Moo: Cows That Type*.

26. This theme also emerged in student analysis of data from placement essays in chapter 1.

CHAPTER FOUR

27. Books like McComiskey's *Teaching Writing as a Social Process* and Wallace and Ewald's *Mutuality in the Rhetoric and Composition*

Classroom begin discussions about the ways that knowledge-building can be constructed as the business of composition classrooms. However, their approaches favor continuing the construction of composition programs as multiple sections of isolated courses.

28. As Elaine Showalter noted years ago in her discussion of feminist literary theory, recovery, inclusion, and revision can occur separately or simultaneously depending on the purposes and contexts of literacy work aimed at more inclusive practices.

29. This critique is part of the story of the conflict about reading that informs the institutionalization of the process movement. This theoretical and pedagogical story of conflict is less well-known than the textbook versions of process, and it is one of the main gaps addressed by many people who revise process.

30. Although these discussions about writing have informed certain areas of composition studies for some time, the new faculty I work with have rarely been introduced to that scholarship as they were trained to teach first-year writing in graduate school.

31. For another example, see Min-Zhan Lu's "Reading and Writing Differences: The Problematic of Experience" in *Feminism and Composition Studies: In Other Words.*

32. The repetition of this particular quote in both the chapter about student discourses and the chapter focused on faculty development issues is meant to emphasize the far-reaching implications of these "streamlining interventions" across composition studies.

33. See chapter three.

34. Once again, Dianne DeVore transcribed the tapes, and once again I have edited them and present them here as they were approved by the other participants. No substantive changes were made to the transcribed versions of our conversation, although participants removed some materials and made some editorial changes before giving their final approval for the work presented here.

35. In *What We Really Value: Beyond Rubrics in Teaching and Assessing Writing*, Bob Broad states: "In short, traditional rubrics and scoring guides prevent us from telling the truth about what we believe, what we teach, and what we value in composition courses

and programs" (2). As I noted in earlier chapters, approaches to process, program definition, and faculty development practices that isolate composition teachers and students from one another and from their communities function in similar ways, often by keeping the concerns of first-year writing separate from the concerns of departments and the field more generally.

CHAPTER FIVE

36. Trimbur's essay is an example of such redefinition. As Flynn notes, Trimbur suggests that the post-process movement is not only a repudiation of the process movement but also an attempt to read into composition the material conditions of the composer and the material pressures and limits of the composing process. Later in this essay, Trimbur speaks of a conception of author-as-producer as a post-process representation of authorship that replaces the process movement's composer as the maker of meaning (979).

37. The sentence under debate here comes from Olson's 1998 article "Encountering the Other: Postcolonial Theory and Composition Scholarship," which appeared in JAC 18 (1988): 45–55. The sentence reads: "While Pratt's notion of contact zone has been useful in interrogating how teachers exercise power and authority, especially in the multicultural classroom, some compositionists have tended to deploy it in such a way as to defend a kind of liberal pluralism, thereby subverting attempts to come to terms with the truly colonizing effects of the pedagogical scenario."

38. See, for example, Crowley, Berlin, Paine, Slevin, and Miller.

39. Early in the essay, Worsham states:

> The most consequential aspect of writing—of this utopian struggle to make "really free" places, lives, and identities—involves an understanding of the way that ideology works most efficiently and effectively through emotion to bind us to particular ways of life and to place us in the world in ways that make the workings of ideology virtually invisible to us. (104)

"We" might be people who have reached such understanding, who can articulate it in certain forums, and/or who have this understanding whether they can get people to listen to them or not. Clearly, theory is the thing that gives one access to this understanding, however, so to keep theory away from people is to limit their access to "really free places."

40. For his discussion of value-driven assessment, see Bob Broad's *What We Really Value: Beyond Rubrics in Teaching and Assessing Writing*. For an extended discussion about the ways that assessment "has yet to be claimed for teaching writing" and for suggestions about how to make reading student writing more central to assessment, see Brian Huot's *(Re)Articulating Writing Assessment for Teaching and Learning* (2).

41. See, for example, Bacon, Cooper, DeJoy and Herzberg.

REFERENCES

Adler-Kassner, Linda, Robert Crooks and Ann Watters, eds. 1997. Service Learning and Composition at the Crossroads. *Writing the Community: Concepts and Models for Service-Learning in Composition.* Washington, DC: American Association For Higher Education in Cooperation with National Council of Teachers of English: 1–17.

Aristotle. 1954. *The Rhetoric and the Poetics of Aristotle.* Translated by W. Rhys Roberts and Ingram Bywater. New York: McGraw-Hill.

Atkins, G. Douglas and Michael Johnson, eds. 1995. *Writing and Reading Differently: Deconstruction and the Teaching of Composition and Literature.* University Press of Kansas.

Bacon, Nora. 1997. Community Service Writing: Problems, Challenges, Outcomes. *Writing the Community: Concepts and Models for Service-Learning in Composition.* Washington, DC: American Association For Higher Education in Cooperation with National Council of Teachers of English: 39–55.

Bartholomae, David. 1996. What is Composition and (if you know what that is) Why Do We Teach It? Bloom et al. 1996.

Berlin, James A. 1996. *Rhetorics, Poetics, and Cultures: Refiguring College English Studies.* Urbana: National Council of Teachers of English.

———. 1988. Rhetoric and Ideology in the Writing Class. *College English* 50.5: 477–494.

———. 1984. *Writing Instruction in Nineteenth-Century American Colleges and Universities.* Carbondale: Southern Illinois University Press.

——— and Robert Inkster. 1980. Current Traditional Rhetoric: Paradigm and Practice. *Freshman English News* 8.3: 1–6.

Bloom, Lynn Z., Donald Daiker and Edward M. White, eds. 1996. *Composition in the Twenty-First Century: Crisis and Change.* Carbondale: Southern Illinois University Press.

Bizzell, Patricia. 1992. *Academic Discourse and Critical Consciousness.* Pittsburgh: University of Pittsburgh Press.

Bridwell-Bowles, Lillian. 1995. Discourse and Diversity: Experimental Writing in the Academy. *Feminine Principles and Women's Experience in American Composition and Rhetoric,* edited by Louise Wetherbee Phelps and Janet Emig. Pittsburgh: University of Pittsburgh Press: 43–66.

Broad, Bob. 2003. *What We Really Value: Beyond Rubrics in Teaching and Assessing Writing.* Logan: Utah State University Press.

Brodkey, Linda. 1996. *Writing Permitted in Designated Areas Only.* Minneapolis: University of Minnesota Press.

Brody, Miriam. 1993. *Manly Writing: Gender, Rhetoric, and the Rise of Composition.* Carbondale: Southern Illinois University Press.

Cassidy, Nicole. Personal Interview. Millikin University, Decatur Il. October 26, 2002.

Cronin, Doreen and Betsy Lewin. 2000. *Click, Clack, Moo Cows That Type.* New York: Simon and Schuster.

Crowley, Sharon. 1996. Around 1971: Current-Traditional Rhetoric and Process Models of Composing. In Bloom et al. 1996.

Crowley, Sharon. 1990. *The Methodical Memory: Invention in Current-Traditions Rhetoric.* Carbondale: Southern Illinois University Press.

Cushman, Ellen. 1996. The Rhetorician as an Agent of Social Change. *College Composition and Communication.* 47.1: 7–28.

Daiker, Donald A. 1996. Introduction: The New Geography of Composition. In Bloom et al. 1996.

Daly, Mary and Jane Caputi. 1987. *Websters' First New Intergalactic Wickedary of the English Language.* London: The Women's Press Ltd.

DeJoy, Nancy. 2000. Faculty Development, Service Learning, and Composition: A Communal Approach to Professional Development. *Reflections.* 1.2: 30–34.

———. 1999. I Was a Process-Model Baby. In Kent 1999.

———. 1994. Reconfiguring the Grounds of/for Composition Studies: Alternative Routes to Subjectivity in the Work of James A. Berlin. *Mediations,* Fall.

DePizan, Christine. 1982. *The Book of the City of Ladies.* Trans. Earl Jeffrey Richards. New York: Persea Books.

Diehl, William and Larry Mikulecky. 1988. The Nature of Reading at Work. *Perspectives on Literacy,* edited by Eugene R Kintgen, Barry M. Kroll, and Mike Rose. Carbondale: Southern Illinois University Press: 371–377.

Dobrin, Sidney. 1999. Paralogic Hermeneutic Theorise, Power, and the Possibility for Liberating Pedagogies. In Kent 1999.

Eason, Jennifer. Personal Interview. Millikin University, Decatur IL. October 27, 2002.

Ede, Lisa. 1994. Reading the Writing Process. *Taking Stock: The Writing Process Movement in the '90s,* edited by Lad Tobin and Thomas Newkirk. Portsmouth: Boynton/Cook: 31–43.

Ede, Lisa and Andrea Lunsford. 1984. Audience Addressed/Audience Invoked: The Role of Audience in Composition Theory and Pedagogy. *College Composition and Communication.* 35: 155–71.

Elbow, Peter. 1987. Closing My Eyes as I Speak: An Argument for Ignoring Audience. *College English.* 49: 50–69.

———. 1981. *Writing With Power.* New York: Oxford University Press.

Flower, Linda. 1997. Partners in Inquiry: A Logic For Community Outreach. *Writing the Community: Concepts and Models for Service-Learning in Composition.* Washington, DC: American Association For Higher Education in Cooperation with National Council of Teachers of English: 95–117.

Flynn, Elizabeth. 2000. Review of *Rhetoric and Composition as Intellectual Work. JAC,* 22: 977–981.

Gordimer, Nadine. 1995. *Writing and Being.* Cambridge, Mass.: Harvard University Press.

Gunzenhauser, Bonnie. Personal Interview. Decatur, IL. December, 2002.

Helmers, Marguerite. 1994. *Writing Students: Composition Testimonials and Representations of Students.* Albany: State University of New York Press.

Herzberg, Bruce. 1997. Community Service and Critical Teaching. *Writing the Community: Concepts and Models for Service-Learning in Composition.* Washington, DC: American Association For Higher Education and National Council of Teachers of English: 57–69.

Hood, Carla. 2003. Letter. *The Chronicle of Higher Education.* May 2, 2003.

hooks, bell. 1995. *Killing Rage/Ending Racism.* New York: Henry Holt and Company.

Huot, Brian. 2002. *(Re) Articulating Writing Assessment for Teaching and Learning.* Logan: Utah State University Press.

Jarratt, Susan C. 1998. Introduction: As We Were Saying. . . . *Feminism and Composition Studies: In Other Words.* New York: The Modern Language Association of America.: 1–18.

———. 2002. New Dispositions for Historical Studies in Rhetoric. In Olson 2002.

Kent, Thomas. 1999. Introduction. Ed. Thomas Kent. *Post-Process Theory: Beyond the Writing-Process Paradigm.* Carbondale, IL: Southern Illinois University Press:1–6.

King-Grindy, Rosemarie. Personal Interview. Decatur, IL. December, 2002.

Kline, Michael, W. 1999. Teaching a Single Textbook 'Rhetoric': The Potential Heaviness of the Book. *(Re)Visioning Composition Textbooks:*

Conflicts of Culture, Ideology, and Pedagogy, edited by Xin Liu Gale and Fredric G. Gale. Albany: State University of New York Press.

Knoblauch, C.H. and Lil Brannon. 1993. *Critical Teaching and the Idea of Literacy.* Portsmouth: Boynton/Cook-Heinemann.

Kristeva, Julia. 1984. *Revolution in Poetic Language.* Translated Margaret Waller. New York: Columbia University Press.

Lauer, Janice. 2002. Rhetorical Invention: The Diaspora. *Perspectives on Rhetorical Invention,* edited by Janet M. Atwill and Janice M. Lauer. Knoxville: University of Tennessee Press: 1–15.

Lawler, Jennifer. 1995. The Screenwriter's Tale. *This Fine Place So Far From Home: Voices of Academics From the Working Class,* edited by C. L. Barney Dews and Carolyn Leste Law. Philadelphia: Temple University Press: 54–65.

Matsuda, Paul Kei. 2003. Process and Post-Process: A Discursive History. *Journal of Second Language Writing,* 12: 65–83.

McComiskey, Bruce. 2002. *Teaching Composition as a Social Process.* Logan: Utah State University Press.

Meisenheimer, Travis. 2002. Personal Interview. Millikin University, Decatur IL. October 26 and 27, 2002.

Miller, Susan. 1993. *Textual Carnivals: The Politics of Composition.* Carbondale: Southern Illinois University Press.

———. 1991. The Feminization of Composition. *The Politics of Writing Instruction: Postsecondary,* edited by Richard Bullock and John Trimbur. Portsmouth: Boynton Cook: 39–54.

Murray, Donald. 1980. Writing as Process: How Writing Finds Its Own Meaning. *Eight Approaches to Teaching Composition,* edited by Timothy R. Donovan and Ben W. McClelland. Urbana: National Council of Teachers of English: 3–20.

Neel, Jasper. Reclaiming our Theoretical Heritage. In Olson 2002.

North, Stephen N. 2000. *Refiguring the Ph. D. in English Studies: Writing, Doctoral Education and the Fusion-Based Curriculum.* Urbana: National Council of Teachers of English.

Ohmann, Richard. 1976. *English in America: A Radical View of the Profession.* Hanover: Wesleyan University Press.

Olson, Gary, ed. 2002. *Rhetoric and Composition as Intellectual Work.* Carbondale: Southern Illinois University Press.

Ong, Walter. 1982. *Orality and Literacy.* New York: Routledge.

Osborne, Linda. 2002. Personal Interview. Millikin University, Decatur IL. October 27, 2002.

Owens, Carrie. Personal Interview. Millikin University, Decatur IL. October 26, 2002.

Parks, Douglas B. 1982. The Meanings of "Audience". *College English* 44: 247–57.

Parks, Stephen. 2000. *Class Politics: The Movement for the Students' Right to Their Own Language.* Urbana: NCTE.

Pecheux, Michel. 1975. *Language, Semiotics and Ideology.* New York: St. Martin's Press.

Perl, Sondra, ed. 1994. *Landmark Essays on Writing Process.* Davis, CA: Hermagoras Press.

Ratcliffe, Krista. 1996. *Anglo-American Feminist Challenges to the Rhetorical Traditions.* Carbondale: Southern Illinois University Press.

Reither, James A. 2000. Writing and Knowing: Toward Redefining the Writing Process. *The Writing Teacher's Sourcebook, Fourth Edition,* edited by Edward P.J. Corbett, Nancy Myers, and Gary Tate. New York: Oxford University Press: 162–169.

Resnick, Daniel P. and Lauren B. Resnick. 1988. The Nature of Literacy: A Historical Exploration. *Perspectives on Literacy,* edited by Eugene R. Kingten, Barry M. Kroll, and Mike Rose. Carbondale: Southern Illinois University Press: 190–202.

Rose, Mike. 1989. *Lives on the Boundary: The Struggles and Achievements of America's Underprepared.* New York: Free Press.

Royster, Jacqueline Jones. 2000. *Traces of a Stream: Literacy and Social Change Among African American Women.* Pittsburgh: University of Pittsburgh Press.

Ruggles-Gere, Anne. 1996. The Long Revolution in Composition. In Bloom et al. 1996.

Salvatori, Mariolina. 2000. Conversations with Texts: Reading in the Teaching of Composition. *The Writing Teacher's Sourcebook, Fourth Edition,* edited by Edward P. J. Corbett, Nancy Myers, and Gary Tate. New York: Oxford University Press.

Schleppenbach, Meg. 2002. Personal Interview. Millikin University, Decatur IL. October 26, 2002.

Shaughnessey, Mina. 1977. *Errors and Expectations: A Guide For the Teacher of Basic Writing.* New York: Oxford University Press.

Shor, Ira. 1992. *Empowering Education: Critical Teaching For Social Change.* Chicago: University of Chicago Press.

Showalter, Elaine, ed. 1985. Introduction. *The New Feminist Criticism: Essays on Literature and Theory.* New York: Pantheon Books.

Slevin, James F. 2001. *Introducing English: Essays in the Intellectual Work of Composition.* Pittsburgh: University of Pittsburgh Press.

Sowinska, Suzanne. 1993. Yer Own Motha Wouldna Reckanized Ya: Surviving an Apprenticeship in the Knowledge Factory. *Working Class Women in the Academy: Laborers in the Knowledge Factory,* edited by Michelle M. Tokarczyk and Elizabeth A. Fay. Amherst: University of Massachusetts Press: 148–161.

Spellmeyer, Kurt. 1996. Inventing the University Student. In Bloom et al. 1996.

———. 1993. *Common Ground: Dialogue, Understanding, and the Teaching of Composition.* Englewood Cliffs, NJ: Prentice Hall.

Steinem, Gloria. 1994. *Moving Beyond Words.* New York: Simon and Schuster.

Swearingen, C. Jan. 2002. Rhetoric and Composition as a Coherent Intellectual Discipline. In Olson 2002.

Tobin, Lad. 1994. How the Writing Process Was Born—And Other Conversion Narratives. *Taking Stock: The Writing Process Movement in the '90s,* edited by Lad Tobin and Thomas Newkirk. Portsmouth: Boynton/Cook: 1–14.

Trimbur, John. 1994. Taking the Social Turn: Teaching Writing Post Process. *College Composition and Communication,* 45.1: 108–118.

———. 1996. Writing Instruction and the Politics of Professionalization. In Bloom et al. 1996.

———. 2000. Delivering the Message: Typography and the Materaility of Writing. In Olson 2002.

Wallace, David L. and Helen Rothschild Ewald. 2000. *Mutuality in the Rhetoric and Composition Classroom.* Carbondale: Southern Illinois University Press.

Welty, Eudora. 1983. *One Writer's Beginnings.* New York: Warner Books.

Williams, Raymond. 1991. *Writing in Society.* London: Verso.

Wolf, Naomi. 1991. *The Beauty Myth: How Images of Beauty are Used Against Women.* New York: William Morrow.

Woolf, Virginia. 1929. *A Room of One's Own.* New York: Harcourt Brace Jovanovich.

Worsham, Lynn. 2002. Coming to Terms: Theory, Writing, Politics. In Olson 2002.

INDEX